PERGAMON INSTITUTE OF ENGLISH (OXFORD)

Language Teaching Methodology Series

PRESS AHEAD

A teachers' guide to the use of
newspapers in English language
teaching

Other titles of interest

BADDOCK, Barry J. *Scoop!* Newspaper materials for English language practice

CHRISTISON, Mary Ann and Sharron Bassano. *Look Who's Talking.* A guide to the development of successful conversation groups

FORD, Carol, Ann Silverman and David Haines. *Cultural Encounters.* What to do and say in social situations in English

LEE, W. R. *Study Dictionary of Social English*

OLSEN, Judy E. Winn-Bell. *Communication Starters.* Techniques for the language classroom

See also the quarterly *World Language English: The International Teachers' Journal of English as a World Language* (free sample copy available on request)

PRESS AHEAD

A teachers' guide to the use of newspapers in English language teaching

BARRY J. BADDOCK

*Associação Luso-Britanica
do Porto, Portugal*

Pergamon Press

Oxford · New York · Toronto · Sydney · Paris · Frankfurt

U.K.	Pergamon Press Ltd., Headington Hill Hall, Oxford OX3 0BW, England
U.S.A.	Pergamon Press Inc., Maxwell House, Fairview Park, Elmsford, New York 10523, U.S.A.
CANADA	Pergamon Press Canada Ltd., Suite 104, 150 Consumers Road, Willowdale, Ontario M2J 1P9, Canada
AUSTRALIA	Pergamon Press (Aust.) Pty. Ltd., P.O. Box 544, Potts Point, N.S.W. 2011, Australia
FRANCE	Pergamon Press SARL, 24 rue des Ecoles, 75240 Paris, Cedex 05, France
FEDERAL REPUBLIC OF GERMANY	Pergamon Press GmbH, Hammerweg 6, D-6242 Kronberg-Taunus, Federal Republic of Germany

Copyright © 1983 Pergamon Press Ltd.

First edition 1983

Library of Congress Cataloging in Publication Data

Baddock, Barry.
Press Ahead.
(Language teaching methodology series)
Bibliography: p.
1. English language — Study and teaching — Foreign speakers. 2. Newspapers in education. I. Title.
II. Series.
PE1128.A2B26 1983   428.6′4′071   83-13274

British Library Cataloguing in Publication Data

Baddock, Barry J.
Press Ahead: a teachers' guide to the use of newspapers in English language teaching. –
(Language teaching methodology series)
1. English language — Study and teaching — Foreign students 2. Newspapers in education
I. Title   II. Series
428.2′4′07   PE1128
ISBN 0-08-029441-3

Printed in Great Britain by A. Wheaton & Co. Ltd., Exeter

Acknowledgements

Thanks are due to the following for their permission to reproduce certain items: John Anscomb (cartoon, page 41), *Private Eye* (Maclachlan cartoons, pages 46–47), BMW AG (ad, page 71), British Telecom (ads, page 72), Police Careers (ad, page 91), *Topeka Capital-Journal* (ad, page 96), Dateline International (ad, page 97), *Daily Express* (Target, page 98) and *Daily Star* (Stepword, page 98).

Contents

Introduction

Most English teachers have used newspapers in class from time to time. But many have not done so regularly, either because EFL studies have traditionally led on to the study of literature or because they felt that 'newspaper language' was too difficult for foreign students. Until about the mid-1960s, the practical skill of getting information out of the popular press was very largely neglected in EFL classes. What newspaper work was done normally focused on newspaper articles (to the neglect of other components like advertisements and crosswords), generally within the strict context of reading comprehension.

Since the mid-1960s, however, there has been a growing acceptance of 'authentic materials' in EFL classrooms — that is, materials produced by native speakers for native speakers' use. And students have been using such materials from quite early stages in their learning process — a departure from the strict grammar progression of earlier teaching methods. Newspapers are now widely accepted as valid language-learning instruments, whose diversity of interesting contemporary text-types includes not only journalists' prose but items like cartoons, small ads, readers' letters and weather reports, all of which are seen and used by native speakers daily. Added to this, language teaching has reached beyond its traditional linguistic limits, since it has become more and more clear that a foreign language can be successfully learned only when it is studied in its cultural context. 'Culture' is used here in its wider sense: the values, norms, habits, psychology and life-style of a nation. Newspapers communicate the value system of a country and there are few better means of bringing the foreign culture into the classroom. And, besides this, they are still an inexpensive resource in a market which has become ever more expensive and technological.

Primarily, newspapers are valuable to language students and native speakers as carriers of news. But they are valuable to language students for other reasons too:

1. *Language learning*: newspapers contain a variety of text-types and these contextualized language styles all provide good materials for language practice. Often they are the teacher's and students' only source of new language.

2. *Developing communicative skills*: after deducing knowledge of the language features of different newspaper components, students can then use this knowledge in a range of communication activities, to exercise speaking, listening, reading and writing skills.

3. *Cultural learning*: photographs, advertisements, articles, cartoons, letters to the editor – all can be used to teach something about the psychology, habits and values of people in the foreign culture: how people live, what they wear, do and think and what issues they feel are important.

4. *Interest and motivation*: because newspapers contain so much variety and because they contain stimulating (often visual) material, they are interesting for students to work with.

Apart from these reasons for bringing newspapers into class, there is a further, perhaps overriding, reason: students will need to use and understand newspapers if they ever have to study, work or live in the foreign country. The study of newspapers is, without doubt, for many language students an important and authentic practice task.

About This Book

Press Ahead is a teacher's manual. The exercises and activities described in it are all based on different parts of newspapers: articles, classified ads, headlines and so on. Many of the exercises and activities appear in their full (student's) format in *Scoop!*, a student's workbook. The teaching manual and the workbook can be used independently of each other, but the teacher will find *Scoop!* a valuable adjunct to this manual since it contains complete worksheets in each chapter, a wide range of visuals and newspaper text-types and useful vocabulary aids. An advantage of *Scoop!* is that its exercises are self-contained, which means it can be used in class without access to actual newspapers.

Each chapter of *Press Ahead* contains descriptions of:

(i) **Deductive Exercises**, by which students are led to work out the language features of the component concerned (e.g. headlines).

(ii) **A Summary of Language Features**, which students should be familiar with before going on to the activities which follow.

(iii) **Activities**, which draw upon the student's knowledge of the language or cultural features he has deduced or learned.

Using this sequence, you can take one newspaper feature at a time, get students to deduce some or all of the language rules operating and help students to summarize them before moving on to the more creative activities suggested.

A word of advice: don't try to cover large units of 'newspaper work' — one ot two features per class would be better. And each time you use a newspaper, select another type of feature. Following the Deductive Exercises, use the Activities in the manual selectively, 'dipping into' this one and then that — for variety, it is said, is the spice of life!

Finally, get students to bring a good dictionary with them at all times — they will certainly need it.

Now — Press Ahead!

Chapter 1
Using the Front Page

A. Deductive Exercises

1. Introduce students to the vocabulary of newspapers by supplying a list of journalistic terms and a jumbled list of short definitions. Students have to match the terms with the definitions, for example:

Headline   A regular article which summarizes the paper's own point-of-view.

Editorial   A vertical section of words on the page; the term also means a regular written feature in the paper.

Column   The 'title' of an article.

etc.

2. Supply front pages from one or two newspapers. Have students identify the lead story; comment on headline sizes and types; locate items of local, national or international news; find ways in which front-page editors tempt readers to buy the paper.

3. Get students to use the tables of contents to decide where to look for different kinds of information, e.g. yesterday's football results, information about weekend events, pages for younger readers, etc.

4. Get students to identify the characteristic features of different kinds of newspaper (local vs. regional? regional vs. national?). To take Britain as an example, the front pages of one 'popular' and one 'quality' paper could be brought in. In a worksheet, ask students to assign each of these features to one of the two newspaper-types:

Headlines containing information – concern for 'human interest' stories – huge, sensational headlines – several reports on political affairs – comparatively little text on the front page – uses short words, especially in headlines – little sensational news – front page used to inform reader, not to arouse his curiosity – presents news in an objective and rather abstract way – lots of entertaining material – long, complicated words, even in headlines – written in conversational, everyday language.

The overall aim should be to lead students to deduce the following general features:

Summary of Front-page Features

The front page invariably carries a lead story, indicated by heavier, larger headline type than for other stories.

Most front-page stories contain objective news. Others are 'human interest' stories.

The page often carries a wide-ranging balance of local, national and international news.

Little front-page space is given to advertisements.

A table of contents is a regular feature and gives page numbers – and sometimes summaries – of main items on the inside pages. The table of contents locates other regular features too (e.g. editorials, classified ads).

The front page always contains about two or three pictures relating to front-page news stories. Cartoons or comics rarely appear.

In general, the front page is designed both to inform and to provoke 'human interest'.

In the comparative kind of exercise described in Section A4 (above), students should deduce features in the form of lists, e.g.

Popular	Quality
Huge, sensational headlines	Headlines containing information
Comparatively little text on the front page	Long, complicated words even in headlines
Concern for 'human interest' stories	Presents news in an objective and rather abstract way
Uses short words, especially in headlines	Little sensational news
Written in conversational, everyday language	Several reports on political affairs
Lots of entertaining material	Front page used to inform reader, not to arouse his curiosity

B. Activities

1. Discussion

Have students compare the front pages of (local, regional or national) newspapers from their country and from Britain or America. Discuss:

– How are the front pages different from or similar to each other?
– Compare the number and size of advertisements and pictures, the amount of space given to local vs. national news, etc.
– What effect do big/small stories or long/short paragraphs and stories have on the reader of the two front pages?
– What kind of news do editors think is worthy of the front page in the two countries? Comment on similarities/differences.
– Examine the lead story and other major news on each front page. Would the same news reach the front page if it happened in the other country? Why/why not?

It students cannot bring in L^1 papers for this, try to have an L^1 page copied and distributed.

As each of the points is discussed, it is revealing to look at the effects of the various front-page features on the reader, e.g.

– Big pictures = an entertaining, but not serious, paper?
– Newspaper title in old-fashioned print = a conservative paper, rather intellectual? etc.

2. Writing and Compiling a Front Page

Have students name their own newspaper and create its front page. Divide them in groups. Each group is responsible for writing one story (maximum: 200 words) with a short, descriptive headline. Groups could select from stories such as the following:

(i) a recent local or school event;
(ii) an interview with a local or school personality;
(iii) a local or school problem (lack of support for a particular school activity? parking laws?);
(iv) a local tourist attraction;

(v) a report on the local or school theatre or library;
(vi) forthcoming events.

You or the students could also provide one or two interesting photographs on which a group could base a newspaper report.

An editorial group of three or four students should agree on a front page layout, choose the lead story and edit (but not rewrite) stories if necessary. The final selection could be cut and pasted on a large sheet to represent the front page.

Rather than turn students into would-be journalists, this simulation is intended to exercise their acquired knowledge about the design and layout conventions of the target culture (what kind of news gets priority, etc.). Further, the simulation gives practice in general communications skills, as well as activating much of the vocabulary which is shared by journalism and common-core English.

During the exercise, you should act mainly as language adviser. In the follow-up phase, your opinions should relate to the arrangement and design of the front page, rather than the *content* of articles and stories.

Roles for the Teacher

feeding lexis and idioms to the groups;
correcting the final versions of the texts;
possibly acting as editor;
possibly ensuring that a good copy is produced for 'publication'.

In contrast to 'Writing and compiling a front page', you could lead students into exercises which involve editing only (i.e. reading, selecting and deleting). Hand out a selection of stories from English newspapers (or items from L^1 national papers from which an English version – not a translation – can be made). Students can cut out their edited stories and mount them as a front page, complete with lead story, pictures, etc. They should, too, write and mount a title for their newspaper.

3. Wall Collage

Sections of the front page are often suitable for a wall collage on a given theme (e.g. transport, crime). Headlines, pictures and lead stories presented in big, sensational format can be impressive elements in a wall collage. Use mounting paste so that the collage can be removed without trace.

4. Matching and Summarizing

The front pages of large newspapers often have a section containing brief two- or three-line summaries of some news stories like these:

If you have whole newspapers at your disposal, cut out some of these summaries together with the full stories inside the paper. Remove the headlines and have students match the summaries to the stories. Later, students can begin to practise the skills of summarizing by reading the stories, writing their own two- or three-line summaries and checking the real summary from the newspaper to see which was more successful in including all the important points.

5. Press Conference

This exercise involves skimming or partial reading, using the entire front page. Students are told they will hold a press conference in a few minutes. They skim and try to remember as many points as they can about the front-page news. One half of the class, who are reporters, question the other half, who are the people being interviewed. Alternatively, the teacher could be the interviewer and ask the questions at the press conference, after dividing the class into two teams who answer the questions alternately to score points.

6. Sentence Building

In pairs, students skim-read headlines and stories, deciphering the meaning where possible, and enjoy the pictures. Then they select one short, interesting extract and go through it intensively, establishing meaning as far as possible. From the extract, the students select one sentence, and try to build sentences on the same pattern, using substituted 'fillers'. This exercise, combining skimming, comprehension and grammar work, is especially useful for lower-level students. The front page could first be projected on an OHP. The teacher could, rather than use worksheets, elicit comments on the pictures and headlines features, point to cognates and important words and ask for synonyms or quick translations.

7. Debate

The class could debate the motion that

Television brings us so much news and information that newspapers are unnecessary.

Here are some points that could help the debate:

— Newspaper readers can decide *when* to read. TV viewers are limited by broadcasting times.

- A newspaper can be read again and again.
- TV news is always current and up-to-date.
- People who read only one newspaper can be too influenced by it.
- Newspapers provide a greater variety and quantity of information than TV.
- TV shows action pictures and real-life drama. These are more interesting and understandable than long articles.
- TV programmes are over too quickly and allow no time for viewers to consider and think about the news.

Alternatively, the class could debate the truth of the following quotation:

> 'The evil that men do lives on the front pages of greedy newspapers,
> But the good is oft interred apathetically inside'
> Brookes Atkinson, 'December 11', in *Once Around the Sun* (1951)

Besides giving vocabulary help with this (*oft* (archaic) = 'often', *interred* = 'buried'), you might point out, too, that it is a parody of Shakespeare's lines from *Julius Caesar*:

> 'The evil that men do lives after them,
> The good is oft interred with their bones'
> William Shakespeare, *Julius Caesar*.

The discussion about the similarities and differences between L^1 and L^2 (Section B1 above) could lead to a debate on the truth of Arthur Miller's statement that 'a good newspaper is, I suppose, a nation talking to itself' (*The Observer*, 26 November 1961).

8. Classifying

Divide the class into groups and give each group a number of articles taken from newspapers. The group have to perform the editorial task of organizing the articles into the sections of the newspaper which they belong to. This means, in effect, selecting appropriate headings from the table of contents. The groups should then report and defend their selections.

This exercise – essentially a classifying task – can also train skimming skills. Imposing a time limit will encourage students to read mainly for 'gist'.

9. Search

If whole newspapers are available, have students seek out news categories which are not covered in the front page table of contents, e.g. travel, science news. As editors, would they include any of these categories in the table of contents at the expense of other items? On what grounds?

10. Postscript

Try to get hold of a copy of a newspaper several decades old. Use it as a basis for discussing changes in front page style, format and content. Are headlines bigger and simpler now? Fewer pictures or more? How much has the price changed – and what about changes in print size, treatment of 'human interest', amount of advertising? What do these changes say about the thoughts, values and life-style of people now compared with then?

Chapter 2
Using Headlines

A. Deductive Exercises

1. Provide a collection of headlines drawn from a particular field. Sports headlines are useful for this as they tend to be striking and unusual ('Laker's Licked', 'David Broome's Clean Sweep'). Where you think sports headlines would not interest your students, use headlines about celebrities or dramatic headlines (e.g. disasters or spectacular successes).

Get students to identify the language features used in the headlines to attract the reader's attention.

Alliteration, assonance and rhyme are devices which students can easily recognize: their immediate appeal is a useful stimulus. But headlines containing familiar names or expressions (e.g. people, places or events) are also good starting points.

This exercise can be made easier by supplying headlines with the accompanying first paragraphs.

Alternatively, students themselves could select headlines which interest them, and these could be studied.

2. Have students study selected headlines in order to deduce the language 'rules' which operate. Ask

(i) What kinds of words are omitted?
(ii) How do headlines refer to (a) past, (b) present, (c) future time? What grammatical devices do they use?
(iii) How are passive forms expressed?
(iv) What do particular kinds of punctuation seem to signify in headlines?
(v) What unusual words (i.e. not used in normal speech) can you find? Why do you think they are used?

With your help, students should be able to formulate some of the following 'rules':

Summary of Headline Language Features

(i) *Deletions*

Omission of articles, personal pronouns, *this/that* (where no serious ambiguity results):

MAYOR JACKLIN HIRES BROTHER	=	Mayor Jacking has hired his brother
POPE VISITS FLOOD ZONE	=	The Pope has visited a/the flood zone

(ii) *Reduced verb forms*

(a) Past participle (form)   = passive (meaning)

DEVON VILLAGE TERRORIZED	=	A Devon village *has been* terrorized
HAIG PRAISED BY PEACE COMMISSION	=	(General) Haig *has been* praised by the Peace Commission

(b) Infinitive (form)   = future (meaning)

OPERA COMPANY TO TOUR SWEDEN	=	An opera company *is to* tour Sweden
SCHOOLS COUNCIL TO BAN VIDEO GAMES	=	The Schools Council *will* ban video games

(c) Simple present (form)   = past (meaning)

HOPES RISE FOR HOSTAGES	=	Hopes *have risen* for (some) hostages
ISRAELI GENERAL DISMISSED	=	An Israeli General *has been dismissed*

(d) Continuous participle (form)   = present (meaning)

DEMOCRATS GAINING IN POLLS	=	The Democrats *are* gaining in (opinion) polls
MARINES AWAITING GO-AHEAD	=	The Marines *are* awaiting a go-ahead

(iii) *Acronyms and abbreviations*

REVIVAL PLAN FOR UNO	=	There is a revival plan for the *United Nations Organization*
NZ ROW OVER JOBS FOR VETS	=	There is a row in *New Zealand* over jobs for veterans

(iv) *Premodified noun phrases*

Especially where post-modification would use more space:

FALKLANDS PEACE HOPE	=	There is *hope for peace* in the Falkland Islands
KIDNAP JUDGE WINS BRAVERY MEDAL	=	A judge *who had been kidnapped* has won a *medal for his bravery*

(v) *Space-saving punctuation*

Quotations, cause/effect relations and questions are often signified through punctuation:

FOWLER : 'BOSTON MUST WIN'	=	(A Mr) Fowler *has declared that* Boston must win
FACTORY CLOSES – 6,000 JOBLESS	=	A factory has closed and *caused 6,000 people to lose their jobs*
DRUG REPORT: TEENAGERS PREFER BOOZE	=	A report on drugs *has revealed that* teenagers prefer booze (i.e. alcohol)

(vi) *'Short-words-for-long'*

In order to save space, short monosyllabic verbs, nouns and adjectives are preferred over longer, more colloquial expressions, e.g.

aide	: 'assistant'	*quiz*	:	'question, interrogate'
cut	: 'reduce, reduction'	*face*	:	'have to undergo'
spark	: 'cause, initiate'	*pact*	:	'agreement, contract'
slam	: 'criticize'	*drive*	:	'campaign'
rap	: 'reprimand'	*clash*	:	'fight, disagree'
probe	: 'investigate'	*curb*	:	'limit, halt'
spur	: 'move ahead'	*host*	:	'entertain'
weigh	: 'consider'			

B. Activities

1. Using the Dictionary

Select some headlines which are examples of the 'short-words-for-long' rule (above) and circle the word concerned, e.g. EX-CONVICT IN ELECTION BID. Have students seek out the various meanings of BID in the dictionary and decide on the *most likely* meaning of the circled word. Do the same with the other headlines.

A variation on the exercise is to present the headlines with multiple-choice answers, e.g.

> *For each headline below, choose the meaning which makes the most sense. Check your dictionary to be sure.*

Headline

MILITARY CHIEFS GRILL SUSPECTED SPY

(a) Military chiefs have roasted a suspected spy.
(b) Military chiefs have criticized a suspected spy.
(c) Military chiefs have questioned a suspected spy.
(d) Military chiefs have served a suspected spy.

TOWN COUNCIL AIRS ITS OBJECTIONS

(a) The Town Council's objections have been cleaned up.
(b) The Town Council has discussed its objections publicly.
(c) The Town Council has thrown out objections to its plans.
(d) The Town Council has broadcast its objections on radio.

2. Reading for Gist and Relevant Detail

Provide the opening paragraph of a news story. Have students look for the main point(s) of the story, then write a suitable headline. Then reveal the original headline and have students compare it with their versions.

Sometimes the student versions will be more effective than the originals. But where a student version badly misses the point (whether due to misunderstanding of headline rules or to failure to grasp the main point(s) of the article), this is a good opportunity for reinforcing the work of previous exercises by reviewing what went wrong.

3. Note-taking

An elaboration of the preceding exercise is to provide several (preferably short) opening paragraphs of a news story, have students make notes on them, and then to *use their notes* as a basis for building a possible headline.

(This is a particularly useful exercise to follow the Deductive Exercises described above, in which students are *decoding* the techniques of headline-writers: omission, abbreviation, short-word selection and the like. These are similar to the techniques of note-taking and the exercises are suitable precursors to exercises in which students – now in an encoding role – have to take notes on a news story in order to construct a headline themselves.)

4. Learning Abbreviations

Frequently, abbreviations and acronyms used in headlines are written in their full form in the first paragraph of the news story, e.g.

Separate some of these headlines from their paragraphs and have students match them together and make a list of the full meanings of the abbreviations they have found. At least a dozen headlines and paragraphs are needed for this.

5. Practising Syntax

Show the grammatical structure of a headline in this way:

TWO KILLED IN FREAK STORMS

HEADLINE	TWO	KILLED IN	FREAK STORMS
Interpre-tation	*Two people*	*Have been killed in*	*(some) Freak storms*

Then have students (in pairs) study other headlines and analyse them in the same way. It is useful to include one or two ambiguous headlines in the list (e.g. HEALTH WORKERS PAY INCREASE or FIVE DUE TO HANG APPEAL) and to ask

— What interpretations are possible?
— Which is the most likely interpretation?

After this, present disorganized headlines for students to arrange into their proper order, e.g. BAN RUGBY FACE LIFE FOR MEN or PHILADELPHIA SHOT SYNAGOGUE FOUR AT.

After each of these exercises, the student pairs should say what various interpretations they were able to find. Focus especially on grammatical reasons why an interpretation is or is not possible. It is important to credit acceptable interpretations which don't coincide with the 'right' answer.

6. Writing

Give students a collection of headlines and the first dozen words of the new stories that accompany them. Tell the students that each of them is a journalist and that their editor wants them to choose two stories and to write a paragraph (maximum 100 words) on each. Students have to complete their chosen paragraphs.

This exercise could be made into a guided composition by giving out notes on the content or recording a news report on the same subject.

7. Learning Idioms

Present headlines which contain idioms, together with their opening paragraphs, e.g.

How Albania spilt the beans

ALBANIA published some startling news about itself last week, a rare act for the most secretive (and repressive) regime in Europe. It was announced from Tirana, the capital, that the ever-vigilant authorities had foiled an attempted landing from the sea by political criminals, equipped, said the communiqué, with weapons, uniforms, and 'necessary equipment for disguise.'

SDP WILL MAKE DO WITH PART-TIME AGENTS ONLY

THE Social Democrats have decided to become the first serious party in Britain to manage without full-time constituency agents.

This stems partly from the party's decision to organise on an area, rather than constituency, basis, but also from the severe problems on raising funds to fight the next election at local levels.

BELGIUM AIM TO GO DUTCH

BELGIUM, the surprise team of the European Championship, have a chance to emerge from the shadow of Holland in Sunday's final against West Germany in Rome.

But the skilful Belgians aim to go one better than the Dutch and win a major championship.

Have students try to deduce the meanings of the idioms:

spill the beans: 'reveal a secret'
make do: 'manage with small resources'
go dutch: pay for yourself only (e.g. when accompanying someone at a cinema).

A stimulating way of learning idioms from headlines is to play 'Call My Bluff':

1. Divide the class into teams of four or five and give each team a headline (containing an idiom the students are unlikely to know) together with the opening paragraphs of the article. Each team must understand its headline, with your help if necessary.
2. After five minutes' preparation, every member of team A tells the story behind his team's headline, each member giving a different story. One should be true, the others invented.
3. The other teams (who are allowed to know the headline) guess which member of team A was telling the truth and which ones were 'bluffing'; points are scored depending on right or wrong guesses.
4. Team B report their stories – and so on. This activity generates discussion between groups, is an interesting detective exercise and – most important – teaches striking idioms contained in the headlines. At the end of the game, though, briefly review the true meanings of the idioms (since everyone has been trying to persuade each other to believe false ones!).

8. Pronunciation

If you have access to newspapers, get students to assemble their own collections of headlines containing pronunciation difficulties. Have them exercise these examples from time to time.

Have them collect acoustic items in categories, e.g.

alliteration: a pretty penny, a dime a dozen
abbreviations pronounced as words: UFO, NATO
shortened words: demo, provo
homonyms as puns: Chairman of the Bored, Bear Facts, etc., etc.

9. Discussing and Debating

Where they have worked on headlines in connection with a paragraph or two, students might be interested in going on to know the full story, rather than be satisfied with a fragment. You can exploit this in a number of ways (e.g. giving out the rest of the article as a cloze text for decoding in groups; or in disordered fragments for students to reassemble). But a most fruitful course is to lead into a discussion or debate on the issue.

Even without reference to the articles, the vocabulary of headlines can provide a good basis for discussion. Students can use their headline vocabulary lists to discuss a basic theme (e.g. *strike, go-slow, claim, shop floor, pickets* = industrial action).

The class could also discuss the similarities and differences between British and American headline conventions and those of their home country. Possible talking points:

— Do both cultures use devices like puns, rhyme and alliteration to the same degree?
— British and American sports headlines are relatively more inventive than other types of headline. How true is this of the home country?
— What comparisons can be made concerning format and layout?
— Does a special headline 'code' (e.g. omissions, short-word substitutions, tense indicators) also apply in the home country?
— In which culture would a language learner find it harder to comprehend headlines? Why?

The class could also discuss these points:

— Examine a particular headline. Is its purpose to inform the reader, to convince him or to attract his attention? Or does it attempt more than one of these?
— Many people read only the headlines. Do you often/sometimes do this? How could this be misused by newspaper editors?

10. Postscript

Finally, what about getting students to combine headlines and newspaper pictures in unusual ways? It is many years now since a Russian newspaper compositor made the fatal error of publishing a photo of Stalin under the headline MOSCOW GASWORKS CELEBRATES ANNIVERSARY. Students can be even more imaginative — without having to face the consequences of their inventiveness!

Chapter 3
Using Articles

A. Deductive Exercises

1. Give students one or two newspaper articles and ask them to comment on:

- The headlines and the sub-headings and their relation to the articles: what purpose do they serve?
- The ratio of sentences to paragraphs in the articles: what effect do one-sentence paragraphs have on the reader?
- The intended effect of short phrases in quotation marks, e.g. *University authorities are 'urgently' considering McCabe's appeal.*

2. Show students a couple of subject–verb–complement (SVC) structures in an article, e.g.

Subject	Verb	Complement
The new breakfast-time television channel	will open	in February
Mayor Edwards	has appealed	for calm

- Ask students to find ways in which journalists vary this basic structure in order to avoid monotony and to condense information.
- Get them to find other techniques which journalists use to save space. In particular, guide them to relative clauses, e.g. *Six unions bound by the agreement abstained from voting* and noun phrases, e.g. *Elegant, 40-year-old Australian linguist Roderick Fletcher.*
- Have students locate examples of passive forms and to comment on the reasons for their use.

3. Rewrite selected sentences on the board,

— changing verb phrases to one-word verbs (e.g. *Union leaders stepped up the pressure* to *Union leaders increased pressure*);
— changing inverted reporting verb and subject to normal spoken form (e.g. *'We shall act fast,' warned the President* to . . . *the President warned*).

Have the students examine the differences between the original and the rewritten versions. Find other examples of the language feature concerned and comment on their effect.

4. Have students locate key words, that is nouns, adjectives and verbs used by a reporter in an article more than four times. (For this exercise, all cognates should count as one basic word, e.g. *royal, royalty, royalist* count as three uses of one basic word *royal*.)

Then ask students to find synonyms which reporters have used to *avoid* boring repetition of certain words.

5. On the board, rewrite some of the more 'emotive' expressions from the article(s), together with more neutral versions, e.g.

threatens to cut pensions	*may possibly reduce pensions*
launch an investigation	*begin an inquiry*
sensational victory	*surprising win*
last-minute bid	*late attempt*

For each pair, have students say what new effect they think would be created by using the new expression instead.

6. What personal details about individuals are mentioned in the article(s)? Have students decide if these are important. What effect does each have on the reader? (For example, what is the purpose — and the effect — of the information in the phrase, *Elegant, 40-year-old Australian linguist Roderick Fletcher*, when the article is about Fletcher's new pipe and tobacco company?)

7. Present two contrasting newspapers' reports of the same news item. Have students decide which events/aspects receive greatest emphasis in each article. Get them to comment on the different ways the two articles interpret the news concerned.

Other ways texts could be investigated include:

Graphology

— Explore the significance of variations in paragraph type (e.g. large/small letters; light/dark).
— Explore the effect of pictures accompanying the article.

Punctuation

— Measure the tendency to omit commas in journalistic prose.
— Examine the use of dashes to make short parenthetical phrases (at the expense of commas and colons) (e.g. '. . . a nervous-looking young blonde woman flung a crumpled second note — believed to contain fresh demands — on to the pavement . . .').

Grammar

— Other ways of packing information into sentences could be explored, e.g. different types of co-ordination, subordination and parentheses. Have students decide in which examples complexity leads to ambiguity.
— The average number of words per sentence is higher in newspaper writing than in many other kinds of English use. Have students investigate sequences of complex sentences. Readability is more important than condensing information so complex sentences are rarely consecutive.
— Seek out questions in journalistic prose. How often are they genuine questions? How often are they (i) followed by an answer or (ii) rhetorical (i.e. the answer is obvious)? The use of tactics like questions and imperatives help keep the pace from dragging and can inspire a strong personal reaction in the reader.

— Analyse tense. Which is more dominant — perfect (*walked, was walking*) or present perfect (*has walked, has been walking*)? What effect does this create?
— Investigate inter-sentence and inter-paragraph co-ordination.
— Investigate examples of missing back-referents. These reflect an assumption of shared knowledge between writer and reader, e.g. *Not since the royal wedding have Britons had so much to cheer about*, when no 'royal wedding' has been mentioned.

Where British and American articles on the same news event can be compared, students could also look at

– Spelling differences (*centre/center; labour/labor*, etc.).
– Premodifying genitives – normal in American journalism but not in British, e.g. *Prime Minister Margaret Thatcher's residence*.
– Prepositions in time phrases – often omitted in American reporting, e.g. *About 20,000 people marched through Belfast Sunday to show support* . . . (cf. British: *on Sunday*).

Vocabulary

– Spot clichés, e.g. *keep a low profile, failed bid, drop a bombshell, defuse a situation, dashed hopes*.
– Distinguishing words with factual vs. emotional meaning.
– Distinguishing words used to *avoid* repetition and words *repeated* for rhetorical effect.
– Finding examples of alliteration, rhythmic effects, balanced phrases, antitheses, etc.

Ultimately, students should build up categories such as the following:

Summary of the Language Features of Newspaper Articles

Graphology and Punctuation

– Short (often one-sentence) paragraphs, to create a blow-by-blow effect.
– Use of the first paragraph to expand the information given in the headline.
– Sub-headings, to break up the text rather than to inform.
– Quotation marks to (i) give extra weight to certain phrases;
                       (ii) 'distance' the writer from an opinion or reported fact;
                       (iii) indicate technical or novel expressions.

Grammar

– Long adverbial phrases to introduce sentences, e.g. *Calling for an all-*

out strike to back their claim for a 15% pay increase, Union leaders promised . . .

– Relative clauses to (i) vary sentence structure,
　　　　　　　　　(ii) pack in extra information,
e.g. *. . . . the 57 day prison fast by Sands, who is seeking political prisoner status for IRA inmates.*

These are often condensed by the use of present or past participle (e.g. *. . . Sands, seeking political prisoner status . . .*).

– Premodified noun phrases to (i) pack in extra information,
　　　　　　　　　　　　(ii) create dramatic effect,
e.g. *Many leading figures in world music have rallied to the defence of the world-famous, 62-year-old, now bankrupt Amsterdam Concertgebouw orchestra.*

Title-and-name combinations are often premodified: *U.S. Attorney General Ramsey Clark.*

– Apposition, to save space: *Bury St. Edmunds, a Conservative seat, has never . . .*
– Hyphenated adjective forms, to save space: *world-famous, 62-year-old . . .*
– Inversion of subject and reporting verbs: *said Clark; warned the President.*
– Passive verb forms, to (i) give a phrase front-position and so emphasize
　　　　　　　　　　　it: *Locked in her present conflict, Israel cannot . . .*
　　　　　　　　　　(ii) vary the pattern of active verb forms (which are more frequent).

Vocabulary and interpretation

– Use of 'everyday' phrasal verbs, to make the article more readable, e.g. *made out, turned down* for *deciphered, rejected.*
– Frequent use of key words.
– Use of synonyms, to avoid excessive repetition.
– Selective use of emotive vocabulary. This is especially important in reporting 'human interest' aspects.

Writers can interpret events largely through

(i) the degree of attention given to different aspects of the reported events;

(ii) selection of (especially emotive) vocabulary.

You may wish to have students deduce the language features of newspaper reporting and to use this knowledge in an integrated way. One approach is to get them to make judgements about the kind of audience the article was written for. Take the same basic story interpreted for different audiences by different writers. Ask questions like:

— What kind of social and educational background do you think the readers have?

— What do you think their interests are? What kind of jobs do they have?

— What particular language features make you think so? Try to give examples of words, phrases or entire sentences which formed your opinion.

— Is the reporting dramatic, sensational? Or 'low-key', restrained? Give examples.

— Can you find any snippets of conversation, details of people's age, job or circumstances, or any other elements of 'human interest'?

— Can you find any research details, scientific or historical information, or technical expressions?

— Of the two articles, which seems more concerned with sensationalism? Which seems more concerned with accuracy? Support your answer with direct comparisons.

— Write a couple of sentences summarizing the main idea of the articles. Are the sentences the same? How do they differ? Why?

— Pick out certain words or phrases in one of the articles. Are there any significant differences in the words the other article uses to express the same idea?

— For each article, would you say the writer is presenting a reasonable picture of events, or is (s)he biased in some way towards the subject? How? Why? Compare and contrast the attitudes of the two writers.

— Find examples of imperative sentences, incomplete sentences, exclamations, rhetorical questions — all can indicate a more forceful use of language. What forceful words (e.g. *must, will, never*) can you find? Are

they more frequent than mild ones (e.g. *perhaps, might, could*)?
– Can you find examples of clichés (expressions which are unoriginal and over-used) or strongly emotive words (like *disgraceful, shock, outrage*)? Which article uses these more frequently?

As an alternative to this line of questioning, students could use their knowledge of the language features to practice grammar transformations. That is, they could reform sentence structures (e.g. without pre-modified nouns), or do sentence-completion exercises, based on a particular article. As an exercise in stylistics, students could rewrite individual sentences taken from one article so that they resemble the style of another newspaper.

B. Activities

1. Note-taking

Give students reports of the same (preferably dramatic) news item taken from several newspapers. Explain that they should not attempt to understand all the words, but just to look for the most important points in the reports. Provide a list of questions and have students take notes on what each of the articles says, as follows:

Question	Article 1	Article 2	Article 3	Article 4	Article 5
1 What were the terrorists' demands?					
2 What actions did the police take after the attack?					
3 How many terrorists were there?					
etc . . .					

As an approach to note-taking exercises, you could ask the students to reduce the article to a list of 'the 5 *Whs*':

— *What* is happening?
— *Who* is doing it?
— *Where* is it happening?
— *When* is it happening?
— *Why* is it happening?

As a starter (since news often fails to provoke interest), you could get the students to write something newsworthy about themselves, in note form with 5 *Wh* statements. Then demonstrate how real news articles can be reduced in this way too.

This note-taking phase will be more motivating for the students if they know that later (for example, in 'Report writing'), they have to rewrite an article so as to make it easier to grasp.)

2. Comparing and contrasting

Students should say what they have discovered about the differences between the newspaper articles. This can be done as a group discussion. Allocate one of the articles to each group. Explain briefly the news background to the issue. Get each group to read and discuss their article, including information given and any opinion expressed in it. The comparisons and contrasts between the articles should be brought out in class discussion.

3. Report writing

Present a flow chart of a serious situation (a prison escape? a ceremonial event? an account of a rescue?)

Students should write their own news report of the events depicted in the flow chart.

As a follow-up to this, you could have students exchange their reports in pairs. Each student pretends that (s)he is the speaker from whom the report originated. This provides conversational practice in pairs, one speaker interrogating the other for more information and details, the other deciding how much he really wants to say on this issue.

4. Distinguishing facts and opinions

To prepare students for this, some guided questions might be needed to help them distinguish between objective reporting and editorializing. A good approach is to select one or two points in a report and discuss in detail whether (and how) they could be substantiated as fact. Then take a newspaper editorial, i.e. a text containing both facts and opinions:

(i) Working with students, separate all points into facts (the points that can be proved) and opinions (the personal judgements of the writer). Build these up in two columns on the board.

(ii) Discuss and write down, in summarized form, what the main *proposal* of the editorial is.

(iii) Have students then write two similar columns for another editorial. Ask them to compare the balance of fact and opinion, and to summarize the *main proposal* of the editorial.

5. Questioning the evidence

Have students comment on the choice of words in expressions taken from an editorial. Which of the expressions are literally true in the context? Which are exaggerated, sensational or emotive? Here are some examples taken from an editorial at the end of a military campaign:

. . . the ceaseless bombardment of guns . . .
. . . they performed with honour and brilliance . . .
. . . they have suffered some heart-rending blows . . .
. . . grappling with constant danger . . .
. . . a victory of resource and courage . . .
. . . built on hundreds of acts of heroism . . .
. . . an honoured place in military history . . .
. . . the enemy have endured a terrible pounding . . .

Alternatively, take an editorial about a news event whose facts are uncertain or incomplete (often the case with 'hot' news from foreign places). Students should list expressions in the editorial which are inconclusive or negative, e.g.

perhaps	*X believes that . . .*	*probably*
apparently	*Y may be the . . .*	*did not/could not have*

a future possibility   *Z has not said whether*   *It is suspected/thought/ believed . . .*

How do these expressions affect the tone of the editorial? This, an extension of the previous exercise, forces students to look closely at the actual language in order to judge a writer's impartiality. It is profitable to follow this with an exercise in which students, in pairs, take an article or editorial of their own choice and prepare an oral report. They should research background information, prepare key vocabulary items and present the issue to the class as an oral report. The rest of the class should be encouraged to question them for clarification and to challenge opinions. Class feedback will also correct poor pronunciation on the speakers' part.

6. Composition

(a) After reading a selection of articles – and letters – on a controversial issue (immigration control? penalties for terrorism? age of sexual consent?) student should use their notes and vocabulary list and

   (i) decide what viewpoint they want to advocate or defend,
   (ii) make an outline argument,
   (iii) write a composition in the form of an editorial (maximum 500 words),
   (iv) give the composition a strong, convincing conclusion.

(b) Different types of article have their own style and lexis (e.g. theatre, political reports, scandal). To train ability in stylistic variation, get students to take a mild article and rewrite it in a vituperative, attacking style. Alternatively, rewrite a censorious article in a more natural and easy style. Discuss in advance what lexical and grammatical changes are needed.

(c) To get students to recognize the need for topic sentences in composition, have them practise selecting the main idea of an article and summarizing it in a written sentence.

(d) Ask students to:

   (i) Make up an article or an editorial on a current school, local or national controversy (employment opportunities? a new building proposal? a court case?). Exchange articles/editorials.

(ii) Act as critical editors on each other's work, cutting out clichés and unsubstantiated opinion.

7. Discussion

The ideas and information in articles and editorials (and letters to the editor), together with their vocabulary, are frequently used in language classrooms as bases for discussion. Here, though, are some more unusual possibilities.

(a) The class could discuss which single word best captures the point of a lead paragraph in an article.
(b) Alternatively, discuss the difference between the articles/editorials in Anglo-American societies and those in the students' homeland. Discuss variations in theme, arrangement, style, impartiality and attitude. What, in the students' opinions, are the most striking differences and the most surprising similarities?
(c) Based on their study of English-written newspaper articles, students could discuss one or more of the following quotations:

> 'Journalists say a thing that they know isn't true, in the hope that if they keep saying it long enough it *will* be true'
> Edward Arnold Bennett, *The Title* (1867–1931)

> 'Interpretation is fact and fact without interpretation is not fact at all'
> Cecil King (British press magnate) addressing the American Society of Newspaper Editors, April 1967

> 'Four hostile newspapers are more to be feared than a thousand bayonets'
> Napoleon I, *Maxims* (1804–15)

> 'Though it is honest, it is never good to bring bad news'
> William Shakespeare, *Antony & Cleopatra*

8. Arranging

Split an article into six segments, arrange the class into groups of six and distribute the segments among the groups, one per student. The students have to find the right order of segments without showing each other their individual segments. This requires reading aloud, listening and discussion. Each group should explain the reasons behind their chosen order.

9. Grammar practice

Use an article as the basis for a cloze exercise with only articles or prepositions deleted.

Or: look for ambiguous sentences in an article. Analyse the structure so as to reveal the ambiguity.

Use an article for a transformation exercise (e.g. changing pre-modified expressions to post-modified ones). Discuss the stylistic effects of these changes.

10. Vocabulary development

Build up vocabulary lists under topic headings. Particularly list words and expressions which seem to be 'insider' language, e.g.

Cinema: lead role, Oscar, screened, box office, hit, flop
Popular music: pop chart, superstar, backing group, top twenty
The economy: stagflation, boom, slump, in the red, invisible exports/ imports.

Allow daily or weekly 'open sessions' for helping with definitions. In dealing with articles on a regular basis, students could build up lists of, say, twenty new words a week. You could select recurring words (from the combined lists) for dealing with in the open sessions.

11. Role-playing

Articles can be the basis of recorded radio interviews, involving interviewer, main characters, witnesses, police representative, and so on.

Alternatively, a group of students can role-play the leading personalities in a controversy (e.g. about starting a new youth club near a senior citizens' home – representatives will be needed from the city hall, the police, the senior citizens' home, the youth organization, the local residents' association and the parent-teacher association). The rest of the class play reporters at a press conference with the personalities, asking questions and taking notes. The resultant articles can be discussed for variations in emphasis, style and accuracy.

12. Postscript

Students could write their own articles for an authentic purpose: have an editorial committee select and edit articles either for internal publication as the class 'newspaper', or for bulletin board display. The class, under the supervision of the committee, could organize themselves to cover different aspects of news (school, local or national) on a weekly basis.

Chapter 4
Using Letters

A. Deductive Exercises

1. Give students a collection of 'letters to the editor' to read and have them decide which letters

(i) refer back to an earlier letter or article,
(ii) *initiate* a discussion.

Ask students to list the expressions writers use to do these.
Give them one or two letters to summarize in note form. Ask:

— What is the main purpose of dividing letters into paragraphs?
— Where is the writer's main point or suggestion most often to be found?
— What is the main point or suggestion of each of the letters they have?

2. Give out a collection of letters which end with a question. Students should decide which are

(i) genuine questions, seeking information and soliciting replies;
(ii) ironic or trivial questions, designed to amuse;
(iii) rhetorical questions which are much like statements and require no answer (e.g. *Are we to allow our language to be destroyed completely?*).

Have students judge what reactions the letters are likely to arouse: strong approval? disapproval? interest, amusement or what?

3. After reading a range of letters to the editor, students should be able to list the kind of topics people write about and why.

4. Other features which you could direct students to are:

— What rules seem to govern the make-up of the headings (or titles) which editors give to letters?

– How do writers identify themselves in the text of the letter? How often?
– Given a particular paper, how much bias is there towards certain topics and topic areas? Can any *regional* bias be detected in the letters selection of a British national paper? To what degree do the letters in an American regional paper reflect opinion in areas *outside* the city of publication?
– Take three letters expressing differing viewpoints on the same topic. Analyse their language with the intention of describing in one word the *tone* of the letter: mollifying? aggressive? fair?

The kind of information which students might gather from these deductive exercises is summarized below:

Summary of the Language Features of Letters to the Editor

Theme

While newspapers can vary greatly in the kind of letters they print, letter columns carry a wide range of topics, especially about recent news and controversies.

The topics fall into two broad categories:

(i) Current affairs in local, national or international life. Topics can range from comments on local by-laws and opinions about current controversies to larger questions of philosophy and ideology.

(ii) Personal experiences. The experiences can be humorous or instructive. They might relate to a larger issue (e.g. unemployment). This category includes letters appealing for money, help, volunteers or information.

In many papers, particular pages (e.g. sports; film and theatre; home and cookery) carry their own letters column. This frees the 'Letters to the Editor' column for more general topics.

Purpose

Letters in both categories are written for a variety of purposes: to complain, suggest, observe, criticize, thank, request, discuss and debate.

Because editors aim for a wide audience, they do not normally select letters which

(i) are technically difficult;
(ii) interest only a tiny minority;
(iii) advertise commercially.

Organization and language

Letters can (i) refer back to earlier letters or articles, or (ii) initiate discussions. Both types of letter normally refer back or specify the topic in the first paragraph – often in the first sentence.

Generally, each paragraph of a letter will develop one idea. The last paragraph of a letter frequently contains the letter's main point or suggestion.

Letters to the Editor often persuade or influence by using

– rhetorical questions,
– emotive language,
– humour.

Length

Short (e.g. one-sentence) letters are common. The editor's (i) notion of 'readability' and (ii) editing policy determine maximum length; letters of over 300 words are infrequent.

Other deductions you might lead students to are:

– The similarity of letter headings (or titles) and newspaper headlines: concise, short words, omissions, etc.
– The frequency with which writers identify themselves as having expertise or experience in the topic under discussion (e.g. 'I have served with the Federal Aviation Authority for 9 years, and I was amazed to read Mr. Cudden's criticism of the airline pilots' action . . .').
– The thematic and local concerns in the letters columns of *particular* papers: a comparison between a university and a local paper from the same city is an interesting exercise.
– A range of words for describing tone, e.g. angry, guarded, timid, optimistic, pessimistic, detached, hopeful, indignant.

B. Activities

1. Writing letters of criticism and appreciation

Hand out a few letters which students can study in order to summarize in a few words what each one is criticizing or expressing appreciation for.

For what reason(s) would *they* write a public letter of criticism or appreciation?

Have them write two letters – one of each type. Provide a list of suitable topics, e.g. a response to another letter they have seen or a newspaper article they have read; a new law; a new fashion or trend. Alternatively, hand out a picture of an event or a scene (protest march? rubbish in the streets? a concert?): the letter-writers should use it as a basis for their letters.

As a follow-up to this exercise, you could introduce students to these quotations:

> 'When people cease to complain, they cease to think'
> Napoleon I, *Maxims* (1804–15)

> 'Gratitude is the most exquisite form of courtesy'
> Jacques Maritain, *Reflections on America* (1958)

Ask the class how true they think these quotations are, as far as letters of criticism and appreciation are concerned.

Are many letters of complaint a sign of a 'thinking' society? How many of the letters of complaint which the class have read seem trivial or unjustified? What *other* ways of making serious complaints are valid, without writing public letters?

Many people express gratitude publicly, through the letters column. When is this way of expressing gratitude *not* justified? Look again at some letters of appreciation – would the students have written a letter to the editor in similar circumstances?

2. Reading comprehension

Take four or five letters from a running debate in a letters column. Build comprehension questions – both true/false and multiple-choice – on three or four of them, so that students get (i) some intensive reading and (ii) vocabulary knowledge in the subject concerned. Go on to the note-taking exercise (below).

[Note that, if you deal with a newspaper story in class, it is quite possible the following issues of the paper will contain letters on the topic (especially if it is a controversial one). Use the letters to develop (i) words and phrases in the students' vocabulary list for this topic, (ii) a range of information on the topic and (iii) different viewpoints on the topic.]

3. Note-taking

Following the 'Reading comprehension' exercise above, students should read through the four or five letters again, taking notes *for* and *against* the topic at issue. Check that they avoid duplicating points made by different writers.

4. Composition

After the note-taking exercise, students should use their notes to write a composition presenting both sides of the argument, adding points of their own, if they wish.

In the last paragraph, they should state the conclusions they have drawn and show which side has the stronger argument.

5. Analysing style

Bring in two letters on the same topic, one formal and controlled in style, the other more colloquial and emotional.

— Select certain phrases from each letter and ask students to rewrite them in the style of the other letter.
— Ask for comment on punctuation features (e.g. exclamation marks and dashes) in the two letters.
— Have students locate examples of irony, sarcasm or rhetorical questions in the letter.
— Get them to describe the general tone of each letter.

6. Letter-writing

- Ask students what new opinions or viewpoints they would offer in a letter to the editor on a current topic. They should write their letter in two ways:

   (i) expressing their emotions and personal feeling on the subject;
   (ii) presenting a formal, objective argument.

- To help develop students' ability in these two types of letter-writing, get them to analyse each other's letters in pairs. Each student should try to find badly-chosen language in the other's letter — especially examples of emotional, subjective opinions in the letter which should present as objective an argument as possible.
- To sensitize students to the use of, say, sarcasm and irony, have them analyse the language and tone of a biting, sarcastic letter to the editor. Then have the students (in the editor's role) reply in the same style.

7. Speaking practice

Encourage students to read their letters aloud, as if they were making a speech. Make suggestions on appropriate tone of voice, gestures, facial expressions!

With proper preparation, this can be a valuable exercise in pronunciation, intonation and emphasis. It can be a confidence booster, especially for shy or withdrawn students, and should be approached like a drama activity, with planning and practice of key words and phrases.

8. Discussion

A good way to launch a discussion is to have students (in pairs or small groups) report on a theme or a topic covered by a number of letters to the editor. If a range of papers is available, students can

   (i) identify further themes that people write about, and
   (ii) choose one of them and report several points of view, based on the letters.

The report should take no longer than ten minutes, but extra time can be taken for the reporting students to introduce and explain new vocabulary items.

More general topics include:

— What motives cause people to write to the editor? Does it make them feel important to have their name in print? Or do they have too much free time? Do they want to influence other people? Or what? What do you think are the most frequent motives?
— What point of view is usually expressed? Disagreement with a paper? With another letter-writer? Expression of support for a cause? Or what?
— Have you ever written — or would you ever write — to a newspaper? What about?

9. Running a letters column

Often a controversial editorial or article will stimulate many readers' letters. Select a suitable item and invite the class to write letters to the editor, agreeing or disagreeing, and expressing their individual views, for theoretical publication. The letters can be displayed, with the article, on the bulletin board.

Indeed, students could conduct their own letters column, either as a printed periodical or (more easily) on a bulletin board. (There is little doubt that students' own follow-up letters in published form would make them feel involved and motivated.) Students could be encouraged to write on any theme (public affairs, school, complaints, requests for information, opinions). An editorial committee could select the letters for display. They should decide also on how many days' letters will be on display, when to close the correspondence on a given topic, which letter should receive top billing and what heading should appear over it.

10. The 'problem page'

This is a regular letters column which deals exclusively with personal relationship problems, domestic conflicts and matters of the heart. A resident adviser — usually female — replies in print to every published letter, dispensing advice.

You could use the 'problem page' to have students

– List the kind of problems which occur in them.
– Discuss the meaning behind the coded signatures. They are often idiomatic in nature ('Damsel in Distress', 'No Guts', 'False Front') and students could learn their idiomatic uses. Other examples: 'On the Shelf', 'Jilted', 'Playing Gooseberry', 'Two-Timed', 'Only Child', 'Off the Rails', 'In the Family Way', 'Star-Crossed'.
– Decide what advice *they* would give to a particular letter-writer.
– In pairs, compose 'problem' letters to each other. They can, if they wish, 'invent' someone with a problem – and write as if *they* were the person.

Students then exchange letters and write appropriate *replies* to each other.

– As an alternative, you could take a sample or two of the kind of 'confidential' reply which often appears: that is, a published reply without the original letter, e.g.

CONFIDENTIAL (To 'Worried' of Hays, Kansas):

You say you don't want anyone to know about your problem? But the sooner you discuss it openly and frankly with a psychiatrist, the sooner you'll regain that old confidence and self-respect.

Have students try to write the original letter.

– After writing their own replies to a few 'problem' letters, students could read their replies aloud, using an appropriate tone of voice (soothing? sharp? sympathetic? practical and businesslike? reassuring?).

To extend this exercise, students (in pairs) could tape-record both the letter and the reply. This may lead to comic exaggeration of tone of voice – this can be entertaining and is no bad thing from a practice point of view!

– If possible, show students some 'problem page' letters from an earlier era. Compare them with the 'problem page' letters students have seen. What changes does the comparison reveal, e.g. in the use of language or the topics?

– Discuss:

(i) What kinds of personal of family problems is it impossible for the 'problem page' to deal with?

(ii) Whether students have something like the 'problem page' in the newspapers of their own country. Are the topics and concerns different?

11. Postscript

Why not start a collection (in scrapbook form or on the bulletin board) of odd or amusing letters.

If you have access to a particular paper regularly, this can be an exercise in reading comprehension *and* search skills, since it is necessary often to bring together the letter and another item to which it refers. Examples:

Princess of Wales expects baby in June

THE Princess of Wales is expecting a baby, it was announced by Buckingham Palace yesterday, 90 days after the royal wedding.

Prince Charles and the Princess said they were delighted at the news, which was given to the Queen a few days ago. Shortly after it was publicly announced by Buckingham Palace yesterday morning, they attended a lunch given by the Corporation of London.

The Lord Mayor of London, Colonel Sir Ronald Gardner Thorpe, told them: "Babies are bits of stardust blown from the hand of God."

The baby will be delivered by the Queen's gynaecologist, George Pinker, who also at the birth of Prin- children in the St Mary's On a rd in st

Sir,—I would like to thank the Lord Mayor of London for his comment (Guardian, November 6) concerning the royal pregnancy. I always thought babies were found under gooseberry bushes—
Sincerely,
Barry Hobbs
Sheffield.

Chapter 5
Using Cartoon and Comic Strips

A. Deductive Exercises

1. Present a collection of cartoons and strips whose captions include verb phrases (e.g. *make out, pull through, hang up*) – a notoriously difficult field for English language students.

With the aid of the pictures, students might be able to deduce the meaning of the verb phrases. To make this easier, add a list of the verb phrases together with a list of their definitions in random order for students to match, e.g.

make out – 'end a phone conversation'
pull through – 'decipher, understand'
hang up – 'survive'
etc.

In the same way, you could use cartoons and strips which illustrate idioms (e.g. *make ends meet, lead a dog's life, be black and blue*).

2. Cartoons and strips are also valuable in transmitting knowledge about the target culture, not only its language. For example, the cartoon shown here illustrates:

(i) that a favourite pastime among children is stamp-collecting,
(ii) that letters are posted in 'boxes' which look like those in the picture,
(iii) various features of dress, hair-style and interior furnishing.

"Why can't he collect stamps like other kids?"

41

Guided questions are a useful approach here, both for introducing new language items and for teaching cultural facts, e.g.

— Who or what are 'kids'? What does the cartoon tell us about them?
— Describe a 'pillar box'. What is it used for?
— The mother and father are sitting on a sofa. Describe it.

3. From a wide range of cartoons and comic strips, students could try to categorize the *subject matter* of British or American humour, e.g.

— The 'desert island' situation.
— Mothers-in-law.
— Henpecked husbands.
— Relations with neighbours and friends.
— Drunkenness, etc., etc.

Alternatively, students could try to categorize *modes* of cartoon humour. For example, Roy Nelson (*Fell's Guide to the Art of Cartooning*, 1962) suggests eight broad categories:

1. The cliché: this involves taking a well-known or trite expression and carrying it out to its literal conclusion.
2. 'That's life': this classification includes those cartoons which cause identification with the reader or exaggerate realism.
3. Hopeless or ridiculous situations: these depict real predicaments; the humour consists in the fact that they happen 'to the other guy'.
4. 'Out of character': this is a popular type of gag cartoon that gets its laughs by showing a character doing something he ordinarily would not be expected to do.
5. 'In character': somehow, cartoonists are able to create a humorous effect by showing people acting as one would expect them to act.
6. Stupidity: the main character in a cartoon misses the point; there is a certain thrill for the reader because he has the satisfaction of seeing what the cartoon character missed.
7. Inventiveness: this type of cartoon often does not need a caption and illustrates a clever way of solving a problem.
8. Understatement: this is a humorous cartoon of a fairly high level; it is often associated with the British and depends upon a choice of words that is not really adequate.

Summary of the Language and Cultural Features of Cartoons and Comic Strips

Many cartoons and strips use expressions from the following language categories:

(i) Verb phrases, e.g. *make out, pull through, hang up.*

(ii) Idioms, e.g. *make ends meet, lead a dog's life, be black and blue.*

(iii) References to people, places and institutions, e.g. *the Archbishop of Canterbury, Fort Knox, Dallas Cowboys, Hallowe'en.*

(iv) Vocabulary reflecting social habits and trends, e.g. *stamp-collecting, fish and chips, jogging, gay lib.*

Comic strips also contain a sequence of action, frequently with dialogue and a range of colloquialisms (e.g. Fine! Thanks! No kidding? What's up?).

Both cartoons and comic strips can contain visible aspects of manners and life in foreign culture, e.g.

(v) Sports and leisure, e.g. baseball, surfing, fishing.

(vi) The environment, e.g. pillar boxes, road signs, shop fronts.

(vii) Clothes, fashions and hair-styles, e.g. sweatshirts with slogans, sports fans insignia, uniforms.

(viii) Furniture, domestic interiors, offices, etc.: e.g. pub bar, kitchen, police station.

In drawing up a summary, it is preferable to separate the linguistic and the cultural features of cartoons and comic strips. You could give two separate sessions to this.

B. Activities

1. Rearranging

(i) Separate eight cartoons from their captions and have students match them together again.

(ii) Collect a number (say eight) cartoons whose *picture* contains some language element — perhaps a sign on a door, or a slogan, or a name on a briefcase. Blank out these expressions, hand out the cartoons (with captions still attached) and write the list of blanked-out expressions on the board. Students have to match the cartoons and the expressions.

(iii) A variation on the idea of rearrangement is to construct a picture (perhaps a wall) collage. Bulletin boards could be brightened with touches of humour in the form of cartoons and comic strips sought out by students. They could surround a certain theme (husband— wife relations? animals? money?). Alternatively, students could take turns to add one cartoon a day to an arrangement of cartoons on the classroom wall – a regular 'Today's Smile' feature.

(iv) Hand out a comic strip cut into individual frames. Students have to arrange them into their original order.

2. Spotting the odd man out

Collect some cartoons which contain vocabulary items on a certain theme, e.g. *cooked food*: hamburger, steak pie, French fries, etc. Add to the collection a cartoon which does not 'belong', e.g. one which refers to 'vitamins'. Students have to (i) find the 'odd man out', (ii) decide what the others have in common and (iii) build up a vocabulary list on the given theme.

Possible themes, common in cartoons:

— Expressions of friendship and endearment (*mate, bud, pal, dear, darling*).
— Domestic slang (*loo, fridge, telly, box, hoover*).
— Exclamations (*Good Lord! Oh dear! Shucks! Dammit!*).
— Expressions for insanity (*bonkers, crazy, nuts, bananas, lose one's marbles, be round the bend*).

The key feature in this exercise need not be a linguistic, but a visible, item (gesture? clothes? type of school or workplace?). The feature could, too, be the type of humour involved (e.g. five cartoons about minority groups, one about religion).

3. Caption writing

(i) Individually or in pairs, students should decide on likely captions for cartoons from which captions have been removed. Then hand out the original captions so that students can compare them.

(ii) Individually or in pairs, students should decide on likely words to fill the last speech 'balloon' in a comic strip — after the original words have been blanked out. Then reveal the original. Which version do students prefer — theirs' or the artist's? Why?

(iii) Another idea is to use a cartoon or comic strip as the basis for an advert. The task here would be to decide what product or service a cartoon could relate to and to find a slogan to fit it, as well as accompanying text.

4. Learning abbreviations

For cartoons with abbreviations in the picture or the caption, give the students letter-blank clues to decipher the abbreviations,

e.g. USAF = U − − t − − S − − − − s A − − F − − c e

5. Learning idioms

Many cartoons and comic strips play with the wording or meaning of English idioms. Select one or two of these, discuss them with students, then draw up a list of five or six idioms ('Too many cooks spoil the broth', 'Look before you leap', 'People in glasshouses shouldn't throw stones', etc.). Get students to discuss and decide how they might use one of them in a cartoon. How would they slightly change the wording to open up a new meaning to be exploited in the picture?

6. Narrating

For this you need three comic strips without any dialogue, like the one illustrated here. Divide the class into groups of three. Each student in a group should be given a copy of one of the comic strips.

Students take turns to narrate the action in their strips. They should describe it in as much detail as they can:

− Where does it take place?
− What are the attitudes or feeling of the person(s) involved in the first frame?

– Describe the changes in their facial expressions and gestures, reactions, changes of mind, as the action proceeds.
– Make the humour of the situation clear to the listeners.

Listeners may ask questions at any time.

After all three narratives, students should show each other their strips. Are they different from what they imagined during the narratives? How?

7. Discussion

(i) Blank out an important visual part of a cartoon and have pairs of students discuss (on the basis of the caption and the remainder of the cartoon) what the missing part could be.

Each pair should report their suggestions to the class. Which are the funniest/most likely?

Then hand out the original cartoon and compare it with the students' suggestions.

(ii) A variation of this exercise is to take two-frame cartoons like this:

Give students the first frame only; have them discuss and decide the possible content of the second frame; and then reveal the original.

8. Find the differences

Make five or six black-ink alterations to a newspaper cartoon. Distribute the original version to half of the class and the altered version to the other half. Have the students, in pairs, find the differences between the two versions – by description only without showing each other their own individual cartoon. Be ready to help with vocabulary, encourage the use of present continuous tense (e.g. *An old man is sitting there; He is wearing a black tie*, etc.), and supply a range of prepositional phrases:

on the right, around the corner, in the background, just beside, etc.

9. Role-playing

Comic strips are useful bases for short dramatizations and role play, especially where they require attention to timing, tone of voice and emphasis. For example, would a particular utterance require a dry, sardonic tone? an innocent, enquiring one? an irritated, touchy tone? Or what? Discuss and rehearse with students the kind of intonations appropriate to utterances in the strip, then enact them.

10. Postscript

After studying and working with a range of cartoons and comic strips, students may begin to doubt whether the reputation of English humour is justified! The class might then debate Virginia Woolf's assertion that

'Humour is the first of the gifts to perish in a foreign tongue'
(from *The Common Reader: First Series*, 1925)

Students could find English cartoons which 'translate' badly into their own culture and language. (Even non-verbal cartoons can be used for this.) Do these examples reveal anything to students about the English sense of humour – or about their own?

Chapter 6
Using Photographs

A. Deductive Exercises

1. Have students carefully study particular newspaper photographs and make a list of features which are different from their home country: hair styles, clothing, urban and rural features, architectural styles, the things people use and have and so on. Guide students to seek out relevant features with questions like:

— Why are these people gathered here?
— Why are they dressed like this? Comment on their clothes.
— What do you think the building is used for? What kind of buildings does it resemble in your own country?
— Look at the car number plate, the front garden, the advertisement, the telephone kiosk. Are they different from those in your home country? How?
  etc.

2. Present a number of newspaper photographs of situations and a list of expressions which (with the help of a dictionary) students have to match with the photographs: four expressions per photograph. For example, if one of the photographs is of a university graduate ceremony, students would have to match it with the following expressions:

Bachelor's degree, students' union, tutorial, freshman

This search exercise, using the dictionary, combines cultural learning and vocabulary learning.

With a wide range of newspaper photographs, you could get students to build up knowledge of, and recognition of:

Hair styles; formal v. casual wear; street signs; architecture; 'street life'; customs and habits; foods; methods of transport and communication; public adverts; trees and vegetation, and recreation activities.

Slide projectors are especially useful for this kind of activity as everyone's attention and enthusiasm can be geared to one picture.

Summary of the Language and Cultural Features of Newspaper Photographs

Most photographs contain few or no language features – place names, adverts, shop fronts, road signs, etc., are sometimes found in outdoor scenes. Abbreviations feature, too, in some newspaper photographs: on road signs (*mph, ped, xing*), on shop doorways and windows (*lb, oz, kg*), on vehicles (*Lancashire C.C. Road Maintenance, UCLA Campus Police*) and the like.

Photographs do, however, contain a wealth of visible aspects of life style and culture, e.g.

(i) Events, social customs, sports (including indoor pastimes).
(ii) The environment (from parking meters to mountains).
(iii) Clothes and hair styles (ranging from casual to formal wear).
(iv) Furniture, domestic interiors, offices, etc. (including private homes and public places like restaurants).

Also, pictures demonstrate the concrete items which people have and use, e.g. coffee pots, electric razors, cash registers, travelling bags, automobiles, canned beer, and so on.

B. Activities

1. Caption writing

Hand out some photographs with blank speech 'balloons' (as in a comic strip) attached to one or two people in them. Ask students what they think the people are saying or thinking and to find suitable words to fill the balloons. (This can be simplified by handing out the photographs and asking students to write speech captions for them (as in a cartoon).)

2. Role-playing

Hand out a range of pictures of interesting individuals taken from newspapers. Students should each choose one, then get into pairs. Everyone should imagine that he is the person in his picture *and* that he is famous. Tell students:

— 'Decide who you are, why you are famous, what *kind* of person you are, how you talk, think and act — and how much you really want to talk about yourself in an interview.'
— 'Role-play an interview between a newspaper reporter and the celebrity and then change roles. Remember, the reporter wants to get as many interesting, even *intimate*, facts as possible for his readers.'

Student 'reporters' could then write a profile (maximum 400 words) of their celebrity for their newspaper (See 'Profile writing', below.)

3. Profile writing

Similar pictures to the role-playing ones (above) are needed for this activity. Individually or in groups, students should look at the pictures, asking themselves where the (illustrated) people come from and what they do. They should then select one of the pictures and build up a written profile of the person:

— Who is he?
— How old is he?
— Where is he from?
— Does he have a wife? Is he a widower? Or what?
— What does he do now? Is he well-off, ambitious, lonely, dull, energetic?
— What does he do in his private life and in his spare time?
— What particular hopes, desires, fears or doubts does he have?
— Try to say something about his earlier life, upbringing and career, including family background, living situation, and so on.

The final profiles should then be reported orally to the rest of the class.

You could have the groups or the individual students work on the *same* picture, so that several profiles of one person are produced. This makes for an interesting exchange of opinion in the reporting stage.

4. Narrating

Students choose four newspaper photographs, build up a story which connects the photographs and then narrate their story. An alternative is to do this with portrait pictures only. Students choose three or four people who are all involved in the same story, work out the story and tell it to the class.

Students could take one picture only and build a written description or an exciting story around it. A certain air of mystery surrounds almost every picture which is detached from its context. The narrators could have a picture

(i) of a person (Who is (s)he? What has happened to this person? Where is (s)he going? Why?); or

(ii) of a scene (Who lives here? What has just happened here? What is about to happen? To Whom? What is to be seen to the left and right of the picture?).

5. Report writing

Present a few sensational photographs taken during or after a dramatic event (race riot? road accident? an attack?). Students should imagine that they were present at one of these incidents and write an eye-witness report on it, explaining the circumstances and causes as fully as possible. They may, if they wish, say who they think was to blame, and how much.

As an extension of this exercise, students could imagine that the photograph was a front-page picture in a newspaper. They have to invent the headline and write the first paragraph of the news story (*not* a witness report of the accident).

6. Cross-examining

Using photographs full of detail and action, have students study them in detail, memorizing as much as possible. After a strict time limit (five minutes), have student A (who still has the photograph) cross-examine student B (who does not) about the details of the event he has 'witnessed'. Then exchange roles, using a different photograph. This can be done as pairwork, with pairs of cross-examiners trying to trap pairs of witnesses into contradictions and errors.

7. *Debate*

After working with newspaper pictures in various ways, the class could debate this motion:

'Newspaper pictures of brutality, violence and disaster should be prohibited.'

One side could try to argue that gruesome pictures are necessary for the sake of journalistic accuracy – not for commercial reasons.

The other side could argue that they offend many people, appeal to a 'circus' mentality and are purely sensational.

8. *Postscript*

Why not collect newspaper pictures so as to build up

(i) A wall collage on a certain theme (people? crime? inner cities?)
(ii) Picture files to illustrate a number of foreign culture features (sport? architecture? fashions?)
(iii) Pictures to illustrate a bulletin-board display of a poem or several poems – again, on a specific theme (*The Unknown Citizen* by W. H. Auden? *When I'm Sixty-four* by Lennon and McCartney?).

Chapter 7
Using Advertisements

A. Deductive Exercises

1. Find advertisements which students can divide into categories according to the main language feature in the slogan: e.g.

rhyme: Don't be vague – ask for Haig (Whisky), etc.
alliteration: Taste the tang of Tango (soft drink), etc.
personification: My name is Fuego (automobile), etc.

Ask students to look through the advertisements, noting particularly how they use language to attract attention. Then have them arrange the advertisements into categories, commenting on the language feature used.

An easier version of this exercise is to give students *pairs* of advertisements whose slogans share a particular language feature and to refrain from commenting on, or explaining, the language features. Have students find a third advertisement to match each of the pairs *and* describe the language feature which they share.

2. Point out some key (i.e. frequent) words used in advertisements announcing money-saving bargains: *free, save, sale, discount, off* (as in *20% off*).

Have students examine other types of advertisement (women's clothes? confectionery? automobiles? cigarettes?) in order to collect key words for different commodities.

Do many key words have anything in common?
Which can be used for many different commodities?

3. Present some advertisements whose slogans employ idioms, e.g.

We'll put you in the picture.	(a studio photographer)
At Pontin's you don't have to splash	(a seaside holiday camp
out to treat the kids.	organization)

Drive a better bargain.   (a car sales company)
etc.

Give students a list of *definitions* for the idioms involved. For each definition, students have to discover the idiom in the advertisements, e.g.

Definitions	Answer
spend money excessively	*splash out*
inform someone fully	*put someone in the picture*
negotiate a good deal	*drive a (good) bargain*
etc.	

4. Students can then go on to deduce the general methods whereby advertisers communicate and persuade, e.g. by the use of illustrations.

Together with selected advertisements, these questions could guide students to form categories of advertising methods:

— Find some advertisements which contain colours. What impact do certain background colours have? What 'atmosphere' do dark blue and purple create? Or red and yellow? Comment, too, on the effect of advertisements using silhouette, shading and outline in black-and-white.
— Find some advertisements which use other graphological techniques such as handwriting. What is the effect of children's handwriting in an advertisement? Or a personal handwritten letter, thanking a friend for recommending a product? Does a letter attract the reader because it makes him feel like a privileged sharer in someone else's intimate affairs?
— Find some advertisements which omit the product's name but emphasise the symbol or trademark of the product, e.g. certain automobile manufacturers. Advertisements for a particular mineral water contain the expression *Schhh . . .*, rather than *Schweppes*, the product's name. With what kinds of products is this technique possible? What tactic is the advertiser using here? What is its point?
— Look at some examples of products being advertised in comical ways. What types of humour are discoverable in English advertisements — cartoons? Odd photographs? Comic strips? Exaggerated situations? Animals portraying humans? How does the use of such techniques 'sell' the product?
— Look at some advertisements showing pictures of young, attractive

women. Are the products used mainly by such women? Do sexually suggestive advertisements ever portray men? Or do they exclusively portray women? Why do you think such advertisements are likely to appeal to both sexes?

— Look at some advertisements which glamorize past ages, old photographs or bygone fashions. What is the attraction of such advertisements? Is the product connected with the past in any way?

— Find some advertisements showing babies, happy children or old people. What kind of products use such pictures? How do these advertisements appeal to people? Why?

— Find some advertisements featuring exotic people or expensive surroundings. With what kinds of things does the advertiser associate the product? What effect does this achieve? Is the advertiser aiming for rich customers only? Is the product so expensive that it belongs only in expensive homes? Or what?

Similar types of question can be asked of advertisements featuring, say, youth, freedom and adventure, science, celebrities, etc.

By means of these deductive exercises, students should be able to form some of the categories which follow:

Summary of the Language Features of Adverts

1. Use of rhyme

Townsend Thoresen — The fleet you can't beat. (Ferry company)
Don't be vague — ask for Haig. (Whisky)

Also: the use of assonance:

Beanz meanz Heinz; (Baked beans)

and:

What we want is Watneys! (Beer)
Taste the tang of Tango. (Soft drink)

2. Use of you/your

When you've said Budweiser, you've said it all. (Beer)
You feel rather special when you smoke Piccadilly No. 1. (Cigarettes)

This feature is often combined with the use of *questions*, e.g.

Are you a Johnson's baby? (Baby oil)
Have you got the Colgate ring of confidence? (Toothpaste)

N.B. *short-form questions, without* explicit use of *you/your*, are common:

Indigestion sufferer? (Indigestion tablets)
Choosing paint? (Housepaint)

3. Use of imperative statements

Fly on it, drive on it, sleep on it, shop on it, and naturally, dine on it.
    (Diners Club credit card)
Try Bacardi and tonic. (Rum)

4. Use of technical information

The new 4-wheel servo-assisted disc brakes . . .
The all-synchromesh close-ratio gearbox . . .

5. Use of key words

Natural things are on their way back. (Guinness beer)
This unique, mellow, yet refreshing, smooth and subtly sweet, full-
    strength white Vermouth . . .

Highly frequent key words in advertisements are *free, new, good, natural, golden, real, rich, unique*. Other all-purpose adjectives used to describe almost anything are:

wonderful   fantastic   fabulous   great   special
sure   fine   lovely   pure   beautiful

Further, advertisers tend to use certain key words for certain kinds of goods. For example, food advertisements:

delicious   crisp   fresh   rich   light

And clothes (women):

style/stylish   smart   elegant   lovely   fine(st)

Compound forms are often used:

(i) *word combinations*:

dewy-fresh (i.e. dew + fresh) (skin lotion)
fast-foaming (i.e. fast + foam) (washing powder)
Also
tangle-free (shampoo), squeaky-clean (washing-up liquid), farmhouse-fresh (bread), coffee-pot-fresh (instant coffee), honey-coated (breakfast cereal)

(ii) *affixed forms*:

super + adjective: superfine (flour)
ultra + adjective: ultramodern (perfume)
adjective/noun + *y*: meaty, chunky, roomy, zoomy
out + verb: outshine, outdo, outperform

6. Use of graphology

That is, combining words with other visual devices:

7. Use of personification

My name is Fuego. (Automobile)
Flowers by Interflora speak from the heart.

8. Use of puns

(i) *rhyming puns*:
A Dutch of elegance. (Dutch cigars)
Say hello to the good buys. (Duty-free shop at airport)

(ii) *homonyms*:
Full board, never board. (Holiday accommodation)
Get a little younger every day. (Younger's beer)

(iii) *idioms*:
With your support we can push the boat out. (Lifeboat Association appeal) (Push the boat out = have a great celebration)
Bouldin's for top class photography – We'll put you in the picture. (Be in the picture = be fully informed)

9. Use of comparatives and superlatives

(i) Belair cigarettes are fresher tasting.
McVities bake a better biscuit.
(ii) This wonderful garment is made from the finest Botany wool.
Wilkinson – the world's finest blade.

10. Use of metaphor

Cool as a mountain stream (cigarettes)
Rich as a tropical sunset . . . (chocolate liqueur)

11. Use of neologisms

Laker Budjets – designed to fit your budjet. (Airline) (budget + jet = budjet)
Getatable Newport – the 10 minutes from anywhere town. (A place which people are able to 'get at' = 'getatable').

Students could also build a list of devices such as the following:

(i) Colours: dark blue and purple for rich, expensive background; red and yellow for happy, joyful backgrounds; etc.

(ii) *Graphology*: for example, handwritten letters or children's handwriting are 'human', personal and intriguing to the reader.

(iii) *Humour*: funny situations, cartoons, unlikely events, etc., are illustrated, to attract the reader.

(iv) *Sex*: pictures of young, attractive women can make the product appealing to men (through association), but also to women (who would like to be as young and attractive as the woman in the picture).

(v) *Nostalgia and sentimentality*: old pictures and old fashions make the 'good old days' seem more alluring than the present. A product will seem more desirable if it is associated with old-fashioned values and virtues or with an idyllic view of the past. Similarly, pictures of babies and little children create a pleasant, sentimental effect which makes the product desirable.

(vi) *Exclusiveness*: the advertisement tells you that the product is only chosen by the very best people – this is why it is rather expensive.

(vii) *Symbolism*: the product is already well-known and the advertiser wants mainly to keep the product's image alive in the reader's mind. This is done by making the trademark synonymous with the product's name.

(viii) *Youth*: such advertisements show young people having a party, laughing, singing, having a lovely time – and using the product. The product is shown as being as desirable as youth itself.

(ix) *The 'latest thing'*: here the advertiser tries to persuade the reader that the product is a new, sensational breakthrough.

(x) *Science*: the product here is presented often by a serious-looking man in a white coat – obviously a scientific expert – who mentions the technical qualities of the product.

(xi) *Celebrities*: well-known people, like sports stars or TV personalities, are shown using the product. The reader, respecting the celebrity, will respect his/her opinion about the product.

(xii) *Adventure and freedom*: such advertisements show people – sometimes alone in the wilderness – enjoying excitement or contentment far from the hassles of the city. The product seems to be a 'passport' to such an escape.

Some advertisements use more than one of these effects simultaneously. Try to lead students to form at least seven or eight of these broad categories.

B. Activities

1. Developing vocabulary

Many advertisements both name and illustrate the article which they are selling. Hand out some of these, having separated the article's name from its illustration. Students have to arrange the pictures and the names into their proper pairs. (Note: the names concerned should be common nouns — *kitchen scales, truck, binoculars* — rather than brand names.)

If a range of newspapers are available, students could look for and assemble their own advertisements containing named items.

A variation on this exercise is to issue a collection of advertisements in which all except one contain named items. This becomes, then, a detective exercise in which students concentrate even more on the vocabulary in the advertisements.

To save students simply guessing at unknown items, it is important that dictionaries be used in this kind of exercise.

2. Analysing neologisms

Have students study advertisements in order to seek out neologisms, i.e. invented words, e.g.

Try a little VC 10-derness. (Ad for VC10 airliner)
Turn your day into a Heinz Souperday. (Heinz soup)
Drinka Pinta Milka Day. (Milk)
Schweppervescence. (Schweppes mineral water)

In each case, ask students to decide what words have been combined to produce the neologism.

An interesting follow-up exercise, combining morphological and semantic skills, is for students to try and create their own neologisms for 'advertising' purposes. It is easier to begin with a particular noun, verb or adjective and to adapt the word to any suitable product, rather than start with a product.

3. Matching

Give students some advertising slogans which are in the form of a question, e.g.

(i) Aching feet? Do you long for sunshine again?
Is your tax man giving you problems? Need help getting up?

Students try to decide what product or service is being advertised in each case.

They should try, too, to comment on the target group of the advertisement. Who is it aimed at? young/old people? male/female? rich/poor? etc.

Compare students' choices with the original advertisements at the end.

(ii) A variation on this is to isolate unusual advertising slogans and have students, in pairs, decide on the article or service they are probably advertising, e.g.

This page covers 4,371 square miles (a full-page advertisement by a regional newspaper's own advertising department)

Before you go back, take a step forward (an advertisement which appeared just before the university year began, by a company selling pocket calculators for student use).

Each pair should report their decisions to the class and explain the reasons behind them. Then reveal the original advertisement.

In these exercises, the student pairs could, after agreeing on likely products or services, regroup into fours. Each group of four should them compare and discuss their suggestions and select one only for each of the slogans. This approach maximises discussion *and* makes sure that all suggestions undergo critical scrutiny.

Dictionaries should be used (for example, to discover the alternative meanings of the verb in 'This page covers 4,371 square miles').

Where a group's suggestion is valid, but doesn't happen to be the 'right' answer this should be accepted. For example, the question 'Need help getting up?' could as well relate to 'getting out of bed in the morning' as to 'getting out of a chair' (the 'right' answer if, for example, the advertisement is for an invalid aid).

4. Seeking connotations

Select an advertisement which features prominent adjectives, e.g.

Galway cigarettes – smooth, easy, cool.

Ask students to consider the adjectives and to think of other words which are similar in meaning, e.g.

$$
smooth \begin{cases} \text{soft} \\ \text{pleasant} \\ \text{restful} \end{cases} \quad easy \begin{cases} \text{simple} \\ \text{relaxing} \\ \text{enjoyable} \end{cases} \quad cool \begin{cases} \text{calm} \\ \text{mild} \\ \text{controlled} \end{cases}
$$

Do the three adjectives still seem suitable for the advertised product? Which – if any – seem unsuitable? Why?

Do the same with some other advertisements using adjectives prominently.

Have the whole class choose one product to be advertised (transistor radio? bourbon?). In pairs, they (i) choose three adjectives to advertise their product, then (ii) list the connotations of their adjectives (as above) and (iii) reconsider their choices and select new ones if necessary.

Finally, the class should compare their choices with each other and defend them.

In order to judge the effects of overuse of certain words, it is useful for students to do this exercise with words like *wonderful, fantastic* and *fabulous*. (See page 57 for frequently used advertising adjectives.)

Which words, in the students' experience, have become overused in common speech? Which words used in advertising seem to have lost their basic meaning?

5. Writing practice

(i) Find an advertisement using evocative phrases (i.e. not full sentences), e.g. *Golden sands. Tropical palms. Rich, milky coconut. Smooth chocolate. The luscious taste of the South Seas.*

Students could rewrite the phrases into full sentences, so as to form a paragraph in a marketing brochure. Ask how their paragraphs are different in effect from the original phrases. Why?

Alternatively, take an advertisement written in prose (i.e. complete sentences) but containing poetic or colourful language. Students could try to reduce this to key phrases. How does the effect of the phrases differ from that of the original paragraph?

The poetic nature of descriptions in many advertisements is obvious. Students might wish to write descriptive advertisements of their own, using similar language. This is best done with luxury products, such as liqueur, rich chocolate, quality clothes and expensive cars. This exercise can be a platform for discussing and investigating the connotations of words and phrases.

(ii) Select an advertisement which contains at least one paragraph of text. Analyse its language with the class, seeking out faulty logic. Refer to the methods, both linguistic and non-linguistic, which advertisers use to attract and persuade (see pages 56–61).

Students could then

(a) rewrite the advertisement putting in all the logical transitions (*and . . . so . . . because . . . therefore . . .*) which are missing – this should expose the advertiser's bad logic; or
(b) rewrite the advertisement as truthfully as possible, presenting only genuine reasons why the reader should buy the product; or
(c) rewrite the advertisement in a satirical way, exaggerating the advertiser's language so much that it contains lies; or
(d) rewrite the advertisement with the opposite intention, namely, that the reader shouldn't buy the product. Do this as a consumer concerned about exposing deceitful advertising.

6. Seeking euphemisms

What kinds of words are avoided in advertising? What substitute expressions (euphemisms) are used?

Marghanita Laski once wrote an article entitled 'Cheap Clothes for Fat Old Women'. How would the students rephrase this expression if they wanted to write a real advertisement?

Take an advertisement using euphemisms (life insurance? skin care? deodorant?) and rewrite it using more direct, down-to-earth expressions. Or, conversely, rewrite an advertisement so as to make its wording less offensive and more seductive to readers.

7. Comprehending dialogue

Take an advertisement which uses an extended dialogue (say, two businessmen discussing a new car, or a shopkeeper explaining a new product to a customer). Go through it utterance by utterance, asking students about

— The speakers' roles and relationship to each other.
— What tone of voice a speaker is using.
— The implication of certain phrases (*No Kidding! I'm not so sure, Just the Job*, etc.).
— What changes, if any, take place during the dialogue (A convinces B? a promise is made? a change of mind?).

A main value of this kind of exercise is that it leads students to think about some of the paralinguistic features of language use, such as the situation, age of participants, probable degree of formality, and so on.

Even advertisements containing only a couple of utterances are useful for this kind of investigative work. It can be done as a teacher-class discussion with questions like 'What do you think is A's attitude to B's suggestion?' and 'What do you think B is doing here — disagreeing politely? making a suggestion? asking for opinions? or what?'.

8. Role-playing

Have students, in pairs or groups, practise dialogue in advertisements, using an appropriate tone.

They could imagine the advertisements have to be recorded as radio commercials — what background music and/or sound effects would be suitable?

The exercise described above — deriving sociolinguistic features of the dialogue — will add to the success of the role play which might follow. Students will be particularly motivated to work on features like word stress, tone of voice, timing, etc., if they know that a recorded performance will follow. This kind of activity is best approached as a drama activity, with the kind of pre-discussion, practice and rehearsal which drama requires.

9. Jigsaw reading

Take an advertisement containing a comic-strip, i.e. a sequence of pictures containing dialogue in 'speech balloons'. Blank out the balloons and present the list of utterances to students in random order. They should pair the utterances with the blank balloons.

It is important to give a fair hearing to any individual or group who have paired the balloons and utterances in a way that is different from the original. In this way, weaknesses in students' understanding of the meaning or logic of the dialogue are best exposed, discussed and explained.

Depending on the learner-level and the number of utterances involved, you might want to leave the first balloon-utterance intact.

To do this exercise, you will need either (i) photocopy machine or (ii) OHP, together with scissors.

10. Search skills

(i) Collect 6–8 travel and holiday advertisements. Train students' search skills by formulating questions like:

— Which company offers a holiday in three different countries for less than £150?
— Where can you have a holiday for three weeks without paying extra for meals or drinks?
— Which holiday combines a visit to a capital city and a week at a seaside resort?
— etc.

From the 6–8 advertisements, students could then select the three which attract them most and give their reasons in a short paragraph.

(ii) Newspapers which print travel advertisements usually collect them together on one or two pages. This is convenient for a group activity in which groups look through the collected advertisements and decide on which holiday they would take as a group. This exercise involves:

(a) *Reading comprehension*: students first have to read the advertisements for gist (What's available? Where can we go? How much?) and then for more detail (Which holidays include hotel accommodation? Which include long-distance bus travel?).

(b) *Discussion and debate*: it is impossible to go to *all* the advertised holidays. So individuals will have to express preferences and resolve disagreements before they can decide.

(c) *Search skills*: the group must check duration of holiday, departure and return arrangements, cost, etc. Perhaps the result of these checks will be a change of plan, necessitating more discussion.

(d) *Oral reporting*: each group should explain which holiday they decided on and why, as well as their reasons for rejecting other strong possibilities.

11. Debating

A possible motion – following on from the *Search Skills* exercise – is that

'Self-organized holidays are far more interesting and enjoyable than packaged holidays.'

Points to consider:

For   – Part of the fun of a holiday is the planning.
         – You can avoid being with people you don't like.
         – Free from the censorship of a travel company, you can meet foreign friends.
         – You are free and not limited by a schedule.
         – You can choose exactly where to go and what to do.
         – No one organizes your activities.

Against – Someone else does all the paperwork for a packaged holiday (hotels, tickets) and you have no organizational worries.

- You know in advance how much the holiday will cost.
- Many packaged holidays provide inexpensive comfort.
- You will almost certainly meet people and make friends.
- Packaged holidays are highly convenient to busy people, more interested in relaxation than adventure.
- A packaged holiday is a good way to visit a new and strange country: the travel company knows what difficulties to avoid or handle.

The subject of advertising can generate a lot of argument. A motion like 'Advertising performs a necessary service to the community' can, with careful preparation, provide an energetic debate. Alternatively, take Marshall McLuhan's statement:

> 'Today it is not the classroom nor the classics which are the models of eloquence, but the ad agencies.'
> (from 'Plain Talk' in *The Mechanical Bride* – 1951).

12. Writing advertisements

Hand out photographs from which students can choose one as the basis for an advertisement. They should:

(i) decide what product or service the picture could advertise;
(ii) invent a name for it;
(iii) decide on the target group (over 40s? women only? the rich?);
(iv) review the language features of advertisements (see 'summary' above);
(v) write the text of the advertisement: maximum 50 words, excluding the slogan and brand name.

Another possibility is to write and design a travel advertisement for the students' own country. For this they should use ideas taken from the travel advertisements in the *Search Skills* exercises.

Alternatively, students could bring (or draw) their *own* pictures, as bases for writing advertisements. Or take a picture they have seen already in an advertisement and do an even better advertising job with it.

The resultant student advertisements could all be displayed in the classroom. As a reinforcement exercise, though, evaluate the language features of each one and get the class to try to fit the advertisement into the language categories in the *Summary of Language Features.*

13. Discussion

(i) The previous exercise could lead into a discussion about the ability of advertisements to persuade. For example, how do the students themselves respond to questions in advertisements? To what extent do they feel influenced by advertisements of any kind? What guides their buying habits? Think of particular products – toothpaste, foods, magazines. Do the students always buy the cheapest product? If not, what causes them to spend money on a dearer product? When buying a product how much do they *know* about it? How much of this knowledge is due to advertising?

Ultimately, you could lead students into building up a series of questions which they should ask in order to evaluate an advertisement. For example, given a particular advertisement,

– Who do you think is the intended target group? Are you in this group?
– What do you know about the product? What do you *want* to know?
– What does the advertisement actually tell you?
– What questions does the advertisement fail to answer?
– Is the information accurate? How can you check it?
– Is all the information relevant to the product?
– What does the advertisement claim the product can do?
– Where and how can you check such claims?
– Does the picture in the advertisement give a true image of the product?
– How does the advertiser use words? To entertain and amuse? To attract? To persuade? To inform?
– What feeling does the advertisement arouse in you? Are they related to the product?
– Does the advertisement connect the product with a particular way of life?
– Does the advertisement seem 'decent, honest and truthful'?

You may want to teach some of these vocabulary items for use in discussions about advertising:

advertising agency: a company that plans and does advertising for other companies

brand: the mark or label that a company puts on the products it makes or sells

code of practice: a set of rules for fair and decent advertising methods

commercial (noun): a radio or TV advertisement

consumer: a person who buys products or pays for a service

image: the idea that people have of a product and its qualities

medium: a method of getting information to the public, e.g. newspapers and magazines, radio, TV, etc.

slogan: a few words, easily remembered, which often appear in large print in advertisements

sponsored: recommended, supported or paid for by someone, for purposes of publicity

standards institution: an organization which tests products to ensure that they reach an acceptable standard

trademark: a brand name or sign that people will recognize.

(ii) Show some advertisements which feature well-known personalities and celebrities, who 'sponsor' the products. List their professions. Discuss why, say, the footballer's public image is better than the film actress's for selling a sports car.

What public image or profession would be best for selling a brand of coffee? A dynamic sportsman? a discerning author? a renowned opera singer?

List a range of products. Students, in pairs or groups, should, as advertising managers, discuss who they would invite to sponsor the individual products – and why. These choices should then be defended in class and finally, the class should vote on which personalities should sponsor products (assuming they would all be willing!).

A variation on this is for pairs or groups to discuss for which products they – as advertising managers – could 'use' fictional or dead characters as 'sponsors'! A couple of suitable advertisements (e.g. a pipe advertisement which features Sherlock Holmes; a stereo advertisement showing Beethoven) can be shown as models for this exercise. Ask students also to write the text of their advertisement.

14. Letter writing

Students could use advertisements of their own choice for writing letters of suggestion, complaint or constructive comment.

The letter could be directed to the newspaper editor, to the advertising agency or to the manufacturer of the product. It should begin 'With reference to . . .', should state clearly the writer's point of view and should end 'Yours faithfully'.

YOU ARE DRIVING ONE OF THE NEW BMW 5 SERIES AT 70 MPH.
YOU ARE 40 FEET AWAY FROM THIS OBSTACLE.
YOU JAM YOUR FOOT ON THE BRAKE.
WHAT HAPPENS?

Find out for yourself at 10.15 on 'News at Ten' tonight when we demonstrate the electronic anti-lock braking system that can be fitted to the remarkable new BMW 5 Series.

The car that's so advanced it's going to take us a whole week to demonstrate all its features.

THE ULTIMATE DRIVING MACHINE

Fool stop

Sir,—With reference to the advertisement for the ultimate driving machine (Guardian. October 21).

"You are driving one of the new BMW 5 Series at 70 mph. You are 40ft. away from this obstacle. You jam your foot on the brake. What happens ? "

The three following cars crash-land into your boot.—

Yours faithfully,
M. F. J. Simpson.
Hillingdon, Middlesex.

15. Postscript

These advertisments for the post office telegram service all depend on the double-meaning of the sender's name.

See how many such messages students can write, using other names. Here are some suggestions:

Bob	Faith	Ernest	Bill	Sandy	Grace	Chuck
Robin	May	Ray	June	Mark	Pearl	Eve

WELL DONE ON
ENGAGEMENT –
RINGO

Say it in style.

There's nothing as stylish as a telegram. And there's nothing easier than phoning it in.

THANKS FOR A
NICE CHRISTMAS –
CAROL

Say it in style.

There's nothing as stylish as a telegram. And there's nothing easier than phoning it in.

THANKS FOR
THE FLOWERS –
IRIS

Say it in style.

There's nothing as stylish as a telegram. And there's nothing easier than phoning it in.

WELL DONE ON
PUTTING UP WITH
EACH OTHER FOR
SO LONG –
PATIENCE

Say it in style.

There's nothing as stylish as a telegram. And there's nothing easier than phoning it in.

Chapter 8
Using Classified Ads

A. Deductive Exercises

1. Present one or two columns of ads, e.g. 'Accommodation' or 'For sale' ads.

Extract the abbreviations (e.g. *AC, apt, p.a.*). Supply letter blanks (e.g. *apt* = ap------t) to help students deduce the meanings.

Lead students to seek out information in particular ads (e.g. 'Ads 2 and 12 both offer hire-purchase terms. Find another ad which does this').

2. Get students to study classifieds in order to find out the grammatical technique writers use to limit the number of words.

Have students analyse condensed 'sentences' (e.g. *79 VW Beetle, one owner, $200*) and decide on missing words. What grammatical categories of words are often omitted? Ask students to find ambiguous meanings resulting from missing words.

Have them examine and comment on punctuation used in classified ads.

These generalizations could be made after the exercises:

Summary of Language Features on Classified Ads

In general, words are included in small ads only when their omission would cause ambiguity or misunderstanding. But it is easy to find examples where the writer, perhaps unworried about the cost of the ad, does *not* try to omit words. So we have to say that these rules are much looser than the rules of other condensed language types (e.g. telegrams, headlines).

1. Use of abbreviations

   Several widely-known phrases can be abbreviated:

   o.n.o.   = or nearest offer   b/w   = black and white (television)

asap	=	as soon as possible	mod cons	= modern conveniences
p.w.	=	per week	PS	= power steering
by appt	=	by appointment		(automobiles), etc.

2. Omissions

(i) *of phrases*

This happens when the phrase can be 'understood' from the context.
Examples:

Sales manager to head new export team . . .	= (A) sales manager (is required) to head (a) new export team . . .
2 x 40″ stereo speakers	= 2 x 40″ stereo speakers (are for sale)
$200 each	= (The cost is) $200 each
Interviewer, 22+, Ashdown area	= (An) interviewer (older than) 22 (is needed in the) Ashdown area

(ii) *of many articles, connectives, prepositions*

'Grammatical' words are often omitted (for economic reasons) where their function can be easily deduced.
Examples:

| Oak table, good surface, slightly scratched legs. £5 | = (An) oak table (with a) good surface (and) slightly scratched legs. £5 (Two articles and two connectives omitted.) |
| I repair floors, Lawrence area, moderate prices. Write John Baldwin . . . | = I repair floors (in the) Lawrence area (for) moderate prices. Write (to) John Baldwin . . . (One article and three prepositions omitted.) |

3. Simplified punctuation

The habit of omitting words results in short phrases rather than grammatical sentences. Phrases are frequently separated by a comma (an all-purpose punctuation mark in small ads) or by full stops. (BrE = full stop; AmE = period).

Examples:

Lost: small, black puppy, white patch on nose, black leather collar, missing in Hill Road area Saturday, answers to name of Bonnie. Reward offered.

Note that a full stop separates "Reward offered" from the rest of the ad. It stands as an independent 'sentence' — perhaps suggesting that this point is especially important in the writer's view?

Experienced drummer needed. 5-man group, progressive rock, some new wave. Road gigs only.

As a stepping-stone to the exercises above, you could get students to look at ads for more expensive 'properties'. These, being less abbreviated, are linguistically easier than most accommodation ads. It is unlikely that many students would ever use such property ads, but their luxurious descriptions generally fascinate and add to their vocabulary.

Some of the vocabulary in the property ads (below) will need to be explained:

freehold: total ownership of the house and the land it is built on
    (abbreviations: F/H; frhld; Freehd.; etc.)
penthouse: a top-floor apartment in an exclusive building
mews: a house with stables attached
porterage: porter's service
mortgage: a form of long-term house purchase
Edwardian: built in the reign of King Edward VII (1901–1910)
period features: original characteristics
ent. hall: entrance hall
recep. hall: reception hall
cloaks: cloakrooms

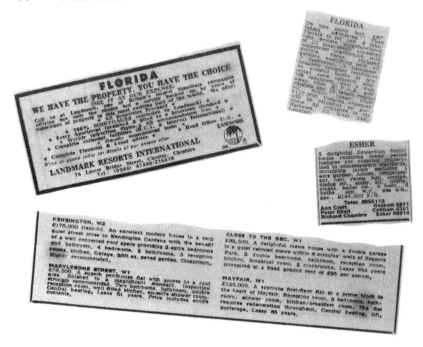

B. Activities

1. Selecting accommodation ads

Give students a range of ads written in different styles according to the type of accommodation – from 'furnished room, £20' to 'delightful Edwardian family house . . .', etc.

Ask students to describe features they would expect to see in the house in each ad, which are not directly mentioned – fellow tenants, furniture, kitchen and so on.

Then, in pairs, they should role-play a telephone call for each ad, student A being the caller, student B being the house occupier. Ask them to decide what kind of person would answer the phone, what kind of tone and response they would use, what they would be mainly concerned about. Each call should end with the pair arranging an appointment. Then change roles.

In addition to this exercise, you could provide four photographs of either

(i) the interior of people's homes (bathroom, living room, anything), or
(ii) portraits of people themselves (potential landlords).

Get students to match the photographs to the ads.

2. Expanding abbreviated ads

Show how a condensed, abbreviated ad can be expanded into a full sentence, e.g.

Unfurn 2–3 BR, new cpting, avail May 1st, 286-5116 aft. 5.

= An unfurnished 2-to-3-bedroom apartment, with new carpeting, is available from May 1st. Telephone 285-5116 after 5 o'clock.

Have students expand other accommodation ads in the same way.

This can be a profitable *and* entertaining exercise with other categories too, e.g. Personals, Situations Wanted. Get students to look for ambiguities.

3. Writing ads

(i) Have students, individually or in pairs, look through a set of 'wanted' ads and show them an order form for placing an ad in the classified columns of a newspaper.

Have them construct a 'wanted' ad for something *they* need in their apartment and decide how many days the ad should 'run'. Set a limit on cost (i.e. students have to calculate the total cost of their ad, based on the advertised rates in the order form).

(ii) Show some 'situations wanted' ads. Have students (a) imagine that they are looking for work and (b) write an ad about themselves, advertising their own abilities and keeping to a cost limit (as above).

'Wanted' and 'Situations Wanted' are probably the two categories that foreigners contribute to most often in British and American newspapers. But you could also practise this exercise with 'Accommodation Wanted', 'Personals' and 'Lost and Found' ads.

4. Telephoning

Students should imagine they are looking for a particular second-hand item, say, a television or a vacuum cleaner. They should

— select five good possibilities from the 'For Sale' ads;
— simulate telephone conversations enquiring about the items (student A = the customer, student B = the owner/advertiser). Students could all act as owner/advertisers for different ads.

5. Practising search skills

(i) Give the class an index to the classified ads pages of a big-city newspaper. Have them seek out answers to questions like:

— Which section should you refer to if you want to learn to play tennis?
— In which section would you place an ad to find a German translator?

This exercise could be reversed. That is, students could try to decide what goods or services particular categories offer, e.g. 'Auditions', 'Rides', 'Work Space', etc.

(ii) As an alternative, select a few ads for intensive study and dictionary work, with questions like the following:

— What could *Equal Opportunity Employer* mean? (an employer who does not discriminate on the basis of colour, sex, race, etc.)
— What might *layover expenses* mean in an ad for a truck driver? (payment for overnight absence)
— Explain 'top perks' in '£7,000 p.a., exc. position, top perks' (fringe benefits, like the use of a company car, foreign travel, etc.).

6. Filling the blanks

Blank out certain letters in small ads and have students put in the missing letters (see example).

WANTED
Van Driver
to carry fr-g-le & v-lu-bl- g--ds.
H--vy re-p--s-b---ty.
St--dy h--rs, sh-rt j--rn-ys.
Exc-----t w-g-s.
Age 30+. R-f-r-nc-s r-q--r-d.
App-- to Britannia Haulage.
An Eq--l Opp--t-n--y Em---y-r.

Another useful approach is to blank out entire words (e.g. prepositions, articles, or selected nouns), rather than individual letters. Supply multiple choice answers. Alternatively, have students select from a complete list of answers covering two or three ads with blanked words.

7. Discussion

(i) Use a pair of job advertisements containing a lot of information as a basis for discussion on these questions:

— Do you think the advertisements paint a complete picture of the jobs advertised?
— What extra information would complete the picture?
— Which ad tells you more about the work to be done?
— What questions would you ask at the interview?
— What, in your opinion, are the advantages/disadvantages of the two jobs?
— Which seems to offer the better prospects for the future?

(ii) Have the class imagine a situation in which newspapers aren't available (e.g. through a prolonged strike). Discuss how the services performed by the classified ads could be continued in other ways. Which ad categories would it be especially necessary to maintain or replace in some way?

8. Cultural learning

All ad categories can be used to deduce facts and knowledge about the foreign culture. 'Lost and found' can be used to find out what kinds of things people place (both financial and non-financial) value on. The

'Personal' columns are even more revealing – for what kinds of reasons do people advertise in the 'Personal' ads? 'Births, Marriages and Deaths' – how do they differ from similar announcements in the students' own country? What differences in attitudes towards death can they deduce from reading ads in both countries? From 'Accommodation' ads, students could try to deduce facts about the size and structure of different kinds of home, meal habits, house values, modes of heating and refuse disposal, etc. Job ads give an idea of which kinds of work carry wages rather than salary, which carry prestige, facts about working hours, 'extras', modes of transport, labour organization and job qualifications.

9. Letter writing

Responding to ads for jobs or accommodation sometimes involves letter writing. Provide a model letter and have students use it as a basis for responding to ads.

10. Ad writing based on pictures

Find a picture of a window or a dilapidated building. Students should write an accommodation ad of the house or flat which it represents. Of course, they have to present it as desirable accommodation without resorting to actual lies!

11. Postscript

Jumble a number of ads drawn from different categories. Have students classify them into their correct categories (e.g. 'Lost and Found', 'Personals', etc.).

Chapter 9
Using Miscellaneous Features

A. Deductive Exercises

1. Television schedules — to make one of the many short, regular features which appear in British and American newspapers — are interesting bases for deducing knowledge about the foreign culture. For example, have students study a TV schedule, in its typical condensed newspaper format, and find out

— Which programmes seem to be documentaries.
— How 'series' and 'serials' are differentiated.
— How many news reports, sports programmes and schools broadcasts are identifiable? How?
— How much can be deduced from a single-entry item (is it a regular feature? a film? a live broadcast? a 'repeat'?).
— What abbreviations mean (e.g. VHF, rpt, pt 10, CBS, NBC).
— What role or function named individuals have (Newsreader? Sports presenter? Film Star? Cookery expert?).

2. Newspapers often print TV guides, reviews and back-up information. An American newspaper, for example, might publish plot resumés of the dozen or so 'soap operas' running at any one time. After reading them, students should try to say

— What they think 'soap operas' are.
— What part of the day or night they are normally broadcast.
— What kind of audience they are intended for.

3. Given printed schedules from both British and American papers, students could try to list differences in the content and organization of television in the two countries.

Interesting alternatives would be cinema schedules, weather reports, recipes, horoscopes, crosswords, career announcements and the like. With cinema schedules, for example, students could deduce cultural facts about the ratio of X-certificate films, restricted-entry films, etc.; starting times; length of programmes; frequency of 'double-features'; prices; special performances (e.g. matinees for children); weekend schedules; classification of films into science fiction, Western, mystery, etc.

Summary of the Cultural Features of TV Programmes

Both British and American TV broadcast documentaries, sports programmes and educational programmes to a limited extent every day. News reports are broadcast very frequently — several times a day, especially in the U.S. where news broadcasts are shorter. In both countries, serials and series are popular. Some of them are produced exclusively for children.

American viewers have many channels (that is, separate broadcasting stations) to choose from, for most hours of the day and night. Several channels transmit late night movies.

British TV, by contrast, normally offers the viewer a choice of four channels, none of which broadcast much later than 1.00 a.m. There are, consequently, only one or two late night movies in a normal British schedule.

CBS and NBC are the two major news broadcasting services in the U.S. The two major British TV organizations — BBC and ITV — each have a news service too. Virtually all TV organizations in the U.S. are independent and commercial. Of the British TV organizations, only the BBC is Government sponsored and non-commercial (and, therefore, does not advertise).

'Soap operas' — originally sentimental radio serials sponsored by soap advertising — are a regular feature of weekday afternoon TV in the U.S. British TV broadcasts soap operas too, but is better known for never-ending twice-weekly serials portraying domestic working-class life.

American TV organizations tend to adhere to half-hour and one-hour broadcasts whose timing is co-ordinated. British TV organizations, by contrast, broadcast programmes with irregular length and starting times.

[Note: Clearly, this information helps students to make comparisons between TV programmes in Britain or America and those in their home country. Probe these differences. You could draw up a list of them and the similarities on the board as they are revealed by the class.]

B. Activities

1. Schedule writing

After the deductive exercises above, give the class an evening's TV schedule from a newspaper which lists all channels locally and nationally available. Individuals or small groups should decide which programmes they would like to watch for the evening. They should

- deduce as much information as they can about each programme they consider;
- note that they may have to abandon one programme to see the start of another on a different channel;
- write their final viewing schedule.

2. Letter writing

Just as many viewers do, students could write a letter to the Head of Broadcasting of a particular TV organization, making polite suggestions and/or criticisms about their schedule.

3. Summary writing

Newspapers frequently print, in conjunction with the TV schedule, a short summary of the films being shown on that particular day. Students could choose three films they have seen recently and write a similar schedule, giving

 (i) the title,
 (ii) the names of the main stars,
 (iii) a description of the plot (maximum 20 words),
 (iv) a star rating (* = average; ** = good; *** = excellent).

At first, you could set a limit of 50 words for the summaries. But you could take one or two of them and work with the class to reduce them each to one sentence — maximum 20 words. Then have the rest of the class reduce their summaries in the same way, so that only the briefest outline of the plot is given.

This could lead on to an oral summary exercise on the same theme: 'the most enjoyable film I have ever seen'. Students could be given five minutes' note-making time, and two minutes' speaking time. They should try to outline the plot briefly and explain why the film was so enjoyable. Allow time for class questions.

4. Debate

Have students prepare arguments for and against the motion 'Breakfast television should be allowed and encouraged', using the following ideas:

For	Against
Banning breakfast TV is unjustifiable censorship. Individuals should be free to choose for themselves.	Additional TV broadcasting will produce a nation of square-eyed addicts.
With breakfast TV, more minority interest programmes (e.g. gardening, folk music) could be broadcast.	Early morning low-cost programmes are likely to be bad, stupid or shallow – no social or educational benefit.
Nobody forces you to watch TV at breakfast or at any other time. You can always switch the TV off.	TV has already destroyed family conversation in the evening – breakfast TV will kill family life entirely.
Breakfast TV would add pleasure to the lives of the lonely, the old, the unemployed and the sick.	Breakfast TV leads to neglect of children – parents will give them TV instead of attention and affection in the morning.
TV has vast educational possibilities, so expanding broadcasting time must produce good results in the long run.	Breakfast TV is a step towards all-day TV: all-day passive enjoyment, armchair life, laziness.
Breakfast TV as a pacifier for young children would be a boon to harassed parents.	Breakfast TV increases the amount of second-hand experience in people's lives: psychological dangers.

Another controversial motion could be

'Television has done more harm than good'

or

'Parents should carefully control what their children watch on television.'

5. Practising search skills

(i) A similar type of feature to TV schedules in the newspaper are theatre and cinema adverts. A collection of these from the same paper can be used for students to seek information like:

— When is the first showing of *Chariots of Fire* on Saturday?
— What is showing at the Odeon on Sunday?
— How much are balcony tickets for *The Tempest*? Is it necessary to make a reservation?
— What films can children see in the city on Friday night? Students will need information about movie ratings for this kind of question:

British Film Institute	Motion Picture Association of America
U : Universal admission	G : General audiences (all ages admitted
PG : Children admitted but parents are warned that the film contains some material they may prefer their children not to see	PG : Parental guidance suggested – some material might not be suitable for children
(15): No children under 15 years old	R : Restricted – under-17s require accompanying by parent or guardian
(18): No one admitted under 18 years old	X : No one under 17 years old admitted

After this, have students imagine that an English-speaking friend is coming to visit. Look at the theatre and cinema schedules and have them decide what they could do on that evening.

You might have students read the schedules as if they were next week's events and write a letter to the friend making suggestions.

(ii) The section of ads dealing with local restaurants ('Eating Out', 'Where to Eat') also provides interesting material for search skills, e.g.

– Where could you be served till 12 midnight?
– Where could you have both French and Italian food?
– At which address will you find a restaurant which serves special dishes on Sundays?
etc.

(iii) A different kind of search exercise would be to have students look for odd items or services in the newspaper and to collect these in a class scrapbook. Students are especially interested in the bizarre or the exotic in the foreign press – palm-reading ads, gossip columns, ads for growing taller, death announcements for household pets, beer-drinking contests and the like.

6. Note-taking

Newspaper weather forecasts can be used, in fact, to exercise all four basic language skills. First, students should study the condensed language of these forecasts and understand the more common vocabulary ('scattered showers', 'bright spells') and abbreviations (Max. Temp., S.E., Mids).

Then play a radio weather report. The main linguistic difference will be that full grammatical sentences are used. Draw students' attention to transitional phrases like 'Turning now to local conditions . . .' and 'For sea passengers, crossings will be . . .'. Then,

– Give newspaper weather forecasts to pairs of students. Student A should have a different one from Student B.
– Using his forecast as a basis, each student prepares a radio report in writing, with full sentences and transitional phrases.
– Students, in pairs, *listen* to each other's report, taking notes.
– They use their notes to write the report in the form of a newspaper forecast.
– These forecasts should then be compared with the originals. Is the original much shorter than the student's written forecast? Why? What space-saving tactics did the original writer use? Abbreviations? Omitted verbs? Did any of the differences result from omissions in the 'radio report'? Note, too, typographical differences, e.g. layout and headings.

To practise a combination of skills (reading, rewriting, speaking), students could broadcast their weather forecasts particularly for (i) skiers, (ii) holiday travellers or (iii) baseball or cricket players. Or they could practise giving oral summaries of the week's weather in review (using the present perfect tense) and of the week's weather currently and over the next few hours (present continuous and future). The details can be invented.

7. Developing vocabulary

(i) The obvious potential of crossword puzzles for vocabulary expansion should be exploited carefully. The following exercise is profitable:

— Divide students into pairs. Give student A and student B different crosswords of the type which appears in popular daily newspapers and uses definitions and synonyms as clues.
— Each student tries to solve the clues in his crossword, then makes a list of the clues he has so far failed to solve (e.g. Across 1, 6, 10, Down 2, 14, 19, 20).
— Students exchange lists and each should be given the *solution* to his partner's crossword.
— Students now make their own clues for the words which their partner still needs. They should use a dictionary and the following clue-making techniques:

Technique	Example
opposites	word: LONGER clue: opposite to *shorter* (6)
definitions	word: JEWEL clue: a type of precious stone (5)
synonyms	word: TERROR clue: fear (6)
blank-filling (a) whole words	word: STAIRS clue: They ran up the _____ (6)
(b) broken words	word: FORM clue: The Drama Club gave their worst PER____ANCE (4)

– Students return the lists to each other with the new clues.
– Each student, after solving as many new clues as he can, looks at the solution for his crossword, uses a dictionary to make sure he understands all the answers and lists new words he has learned.

(ii) A different vocabulary exercise is to list and arrange words according to their frequency in a specific category, e.g. lonely hearts club, cookery.

8. Learning idioms

Horoscopes, another small but regular feature of many English newspapers, are rich in verb phrases (*cool down, get along with, fall out*) and colloquial idioms (*get the better of someone, get things off one's chest*). Blank out some of these expressions and provide students with multiple-choice answers in order to fill the blanks. Alternatively, make a cloze text of the horoscope, with prepositions or connectives missing.

A follow-up to this exercise on horoscopes is to have students with the same birth sign work in groups to read the predictions.

Another interesting way of using the horoscope is to bring in last week's predictions but without the dates and signs attached. Get the students to decide which of the twelve predictions were true of their *own* fortunes during the past week. Then reveal the dates and signs which belong to the twelve predictions.

9. Disambiguating

Get students to search text for an error you know to exist. Encourage them generally to expose misprints, errors and ambiguities. Where a student suspects an error, teacher confirmation of it will add to his/her confidence.

These misprints, errors and ambiguities could be collected (in a class scrapbook or on the bulletin board) when they have humorous results, e.g. 'The Rev. Whelan has invited everyone in the village to sin and pray with him', 'Pauline said that she was suprised to win the beauty competition in the face of so much "young" talent and confessed to being the mother of 93 children'.

10. Recipe writing

Cooking recipes are frequently in weekly newspapers and are (like small ads, headlines and weather forecasts) an example of a condensed language type. Get students to examine:

— The format (name of the dish; list of ingredients; instructions)
— The note-form sentences (omitted articles, auxiliary verbs, pronouns, indefinite quantifiers (*some, a number of*), temporal connectives (*then, next*)).

Examples:

Note form	Full sentences
Blanch bacon in salted water. Drain, dry with paper towels and fry until brown in 1 tbspn melted butter.	Blanch (the) bacon in (some) salted water. Drain (the bacon), dry (it) with (some) paper towels and fry (it) until (it is) brown in 1 (tablespoonful) (of) butter.

Explain abbreviations (*oz, lb, tbspn, deg*, etc.).

Have students practise writing recipes in this form,

— constructing a recipe from a full-sentence version written by the teacher, or
— choosing dishes from their home country and exchanging recipes, if they wish.

Provide conversion tables to help them:

Ounces/fluid ounces	Approximate g and ml to nearest whole figure	Recommended conversion to nearest unit of 25
1	28	25
2	57	50
3	85	75
4	113	100
5 (¼ pint)	142	150
6	170	175
7	198	200
8 (½lb)	226	225
9	255	250
10 (½ pint)	283	275
11	311	300
12	340	350
13	368	375
14	396	400
15 (¾ pint)	428	425
16 (1lb)	456	450
17	484	475
18	512	500
19	541	550
20 (1 pint)	569	575

Description	Fahrenheit	Celsius	Gas Mark
Cool	225	110	¼
	250	130	½
Very slow	275	140	1
	300	150	2
Slow	325	170	3
Moderate	350	180	4
	375	190	5
Moderately hot	400	200	6
Fairly hot	425	220	7
Hot	450	230	8
Very hot	475	240	9
Extremely hot	500	250	10

Perhaps it is possible to combine with the cookery teacher in the school to use English recipes in class and to build up a class recipe book.

Get students to build up their *own* recipe book (in English) and to exchange recipes. This could provide the basis for a mini-course on the culinary arts of the foreign culture, involving discussing and tasting the foods.

11. Reading comprehension

The 'Careers' section of a newspaper contains advertisements quite different in style and content from the normal advertisements (for goods and services) and job ads in the 'classifieds'. A single 'career' advertisement can be used quite extensively to include reading, oral reporting and discussion. Take, for example, the 'career' advert for the Police Force. Have students study the text for comprehension and then give TRUE/FALSE answers to these statements:

According to the advertisement, a policeman

(i)   must make his own decisions, be interested in people and pay his own bills;

(ii) may have to deal with a serious road accident;

(iii) receives three months' training;

(iv) must deal with situations in which people have their heads knocked off;

(v)   will learn to choose between keeping public order and protecting individuals' rights;

(vi) may disagree with a person's opinions and, at the same time, protect that person while he is expressing those opinions;

(vii) may have to go and talk to a married couple who are singing and drinking late at night.

If this exercise leads directly into a discussion about police careers or careers in general, omit the oral reporting phase which follows.

'A policeman's lot is not a happy one', it is said. How do the students feel about this after reading the advert?

If we said a policeman has to be fit, intelligent and of good character, you'd probably think, that sounds just like me.

If we said he has to be a leader, be capable of making his own decisions, and be interested in people, you may think, well yes, I guess I fit the bill.

If we said he might have to deal with a motorway accident involving a tanker carrying propane gas, a lorry full of plate glass, several cars and a coach load of rowdy football fans, you would probably think, me cope with that? No way!

And you'd be right. Because, although you need certain qualities to be a policeman, at present you are probably not even aware you possess them.

We'll have to bring them out. After you've gone through your three months' initial training, you'll have the confidence to deal with many of the situations you could come up against.

You'll learn to keep your head in an emergency, even though those around you may be losing theirs.

And you'll learn to tread the narrow path between maintaining public order and protecting the rights of the individual.

This could mean defending a person's right to speak even though you may disagree with what he has to say.

Trying to talk someone out of leaping from the top floor of a skyscraper.

Or trying to talk sense into a husband and wife having a screaming punch-up at two o'clock in the morning.

Is a policeman able to deal with such situations because he is a policeman, or because he is who he is?

To be honest, there's no simple answer to such a question. But if you think you are the man to make something of the job, send for our brochure.

It will give you all the facts, including details of the attractive new pay levels.

Does the man make the job?

Or does the job make the man?

A POLICE CAREER

12. Oral reporting

After the comprehension exercise (above), suggest to the class that the advertisement tries to paint a realistic picture of a policeman's career, discussing its difficulties rather than its attractions. What attractions does it mention? In other words, why would a young person want to become a police officer, after reading this advertisement?

The arguments for and against a police career could be summarized like this:

For	Against
Strong personal challenge; develops personal qualities, e.g. leadership, decision-making, interest in people, self-reliance; much job variety; complete training provided; attractive pay; a career.	Ofter difficult and dangerous situations (e.g. emergencies, conflicts); uncertainty ('Do I have the right qualities?'); irregular hours (sometimes 2.00 a.m.).

With the students, summarize similar arguments for other careers:

Airline pilot

For	Against
See the world; exciting; good pay; cheap off-duty flights, etc.	Heavy responsibility; danger (crashes, hi-jackers); too often away from home; tiring long journeys, etc.

Nurse

For	Against
Serves an important need; saves lives; make friends; career for life, etc.	Long hours; sick people can be depressing; low wages; long hard training, etc.

Students now get into pairs. Each student chooses a career that appeals to him and writes two lists:

(i) Arguments for his chosen career;

(ii) Arguments against his partner's chosen career.

Each should then give oral summaries of the arguments concerning the *first* career. Then do the same with the *second* career. Provide students with these expressions to help them link their points together in the summaries:

1. *Reinforcing*	2. *Diminishing*	3. *Casual*
To be exact . . .	At least	So
In other words	Or rather	Thus
That is, . . .	At any rate	Therefore
So you see, . . .	At the same time (how-ever)	Conse-quently, . . .
The point is . . .	Anyway	As a result, . . .
As a matter of fact	That is	Because of this . . .

4. *Temporal*	5. *Additive*	6. *Comparative*
Then	Furthermore, . . .	On the other hand . . .
Next	In addition . . .	By contrast . . .
Before that	Besides (this), . . .	By comparison. . .
Up to this point	What's more, . . .	As a contrast to this . . .
At the same time	And another thing . . .	The other side of the question is . . .
Meanwhile	In the first/second place	Instead, . . .

7. *Imposing a new idea*

(i) *Digressing*

    Incidentally, . . .

    By the way . . .

    That reminds me . . .

    Did you know . . . ?

(ii) *Changing the subject*

    Now the next point is . . .

    I'd like to move on now to

    Now, I'll say a few things about . . .

    At this stage we'd better look at . . .

The reports could take the form of a radio report on careers. Introductory and linking comments will be needed, like 'Good evening. Tonight we're reporting in *World in Action* on . . . First, we're going to hear from . . . who has looked into . . .' and 'That was . . . and now on to . . .'.

13. Discussion

(i) After the report stage, the class could discuss whether the arguments for each career outweigh the arguments against. Provide these expressions for them to us:

1. *Giving opinions*
Honestly, . . .
If you ask me, . . .
What I think is . . .
I feel that . . .
In my view, . . .
In my opinion, . . .

2. *Expressing agreement*
I couldn't agree more.
That's just what I think.
Exactly.
That's right.
You've got a point there.
I'd go along with that.

3. *Expressing disagreement politely*
I take your point but . . .
I see what you mean, but on the other hand . . .
I'm not sure about that.
I wonder if that's true, because . . .
You said that . . . but it often seems to me that . . .
Yes, but surely . . .

4. *Making suggestions*
Let's do/arrange/make . . .
What about . . .
I was wondering if we might . . .
Well, why not?
I'd like to suggest . . .
Perhaps we could . . .

5. *Considering one's reply*
Well, let me see . . .
Let me think for a moment . . .
I'll just consider that . . .
It's hard to say offhand, but . . .
How shall I put it . . .
That's a good/interesting/
important question. . .

6. *Imposing a new idea*
(i) *Summarizing* (i.e. retrospective)
In brief, . . .
To sum up, . . .
All in all, . . .
In short, . . .
On the whole, . . .
To put it in a nutshell, . . .

(ii) *Introducing* (i.e. prospective)

I'd like to come now/come back/ go on to . . .

There's another/one other point . . .

Could we switch over/move on to . . .

Now concerning . . .

We should also look at . . .

(ii) If we look again at the TV schedules of newspapers, we find that they are useful sources of discussion topics. For example, the educational possibilities of television – show the class this schedule and advert:

TV Listings

Morning

5:55 A.M.

6 Eruditus

5:30 A.M.

40 Health Field

6:00 A.M.

2 46 PTL Club

3 Tom And Jerry And Friends

4 6:27, Ed Allen - Today's Woman

5 10 Sunrise Semester

7 6:15, The Way We Know

8 6:25, Punto De Interes

11 Sound Off

13 Voice Of Agriculture

36 Yoga For Health

40 700 Club

44 6:05, Health Field

6:30 A.M.

3 News

5 The Morning Stretch

7 6:45, News

10 Captain Kangaroo

13 Richard Simmons

20 Villa Alegre

36 Public Affairs

44 Bozo's Big Top

54 60 6:45, A.M. Weather

7:00 A.M.

2 Cartoons

3 4 8 Today

5 46 Morning With Charles Kuralt

7 11 13 Good Morning America

20 Krofft Superstars

26 Praise The Lord

36 700 Club

40 Captain Mitch Cartoons

44 Fred Flintstone And Friends

54 Villa Alegre

60 Project Universe

7:30 A.M.

9 Yoga For Health

10 Jean LaMotte

44 The Great Space Coaster

54 Sesame Street

60 Family Portrait

Ask the class if they think the TV programme could teach them yoga as effectively as The Yoga Center could. Have them compare

(a) The advantages of learning by TV (no costs; no travelling to class on rainy days; no sharing teacher's time with other students):

(b) The advantages of learning in class (personal teacher–student relationship; opportunity to correct mistakes).

Which of these subjects could be effectively learned through TV?

gardening	cookery	ancient history
giving up smoking	foreign languages	pet care
car maintenance	playing the guitar	first aid
current affairs	algebra	the Highway Code

The students should give reasons for their opinions and you could supply these phrases which they can use for making a point:

In my opinion . . .   Personally, I think that . . .

I believe (that) . . .   The point is (this) . . .
I'd like to say (this) . . .   If you ask me . . .

(iii) Advertisements for lonely hearts can be an especially fascinating item for foreign students. Show a few of them to the class and ask

— Do you have similar advertisements in your home country?
— What kind of people are most likely to respond to them?
— Do you think it is possible for organizations to match people together in the way they try to?
— Do you think there is such a person as an 'ideal partner'?

Then show the class a questionnaire like the one below. They are quite common in lonely hearts advertisements and provide a good basis for discussion:

Ask students to make a list of the characteristics (shy, extrovert, etc.) which they think *they* have. Then ask them to get into pairs and to make a list of the characteristics and preferences which they think their partner has. They should then exchange lists.

On what points did they disagree with each other? Through discussion, they should try to find out why they have disagreed over certain points. For example, perhaps student A thinks he is creative and his partner does not. Each of them should explain and defend his point of view.

(iv) Newspaper ads for cinemas, theatres, entertainments, holidays, restaurants are all good starting points for discussion about students' own preferences and interests. With any of these items you could get students to explain what kinds of things determine their choice.

Furthermore, in respect of these and other newspaper discussion topics, the class could make comparisons between their home culture and that of Britain and America. What items surprise students? Which would not appear in newspapers in their own country?

14. Word games

Apart from crosswords, some newspapers publish regular word games, some of which are suitable for foreign students. Here are two examples taken from British daily newspapers, *The Daily Express* and *The Star*:

TARGET

The
EXPRESS
Word Game

T	I	E
A	**B**	E
N	I	R

How many words of four letters or more can you make from the letters shown here? In making a word, each letter may be used once only. Each word must contain the large letter, and there must be at least one nine-letter word in the list. No plurals; no foreign words; no proper names. TODAY'S TARGET: 26 words, good; 30 words, very good; 35 words, excellent.

STEPWORD

TURN the top word into the bottom word by changing one letter in each successive word to make a different word. We took three steps to get from EASY to HARD. How many will it take you?

EASY
——
——
——
——
HARD

SOLUTION:
Aber bairn bait bane bant
panter bare barn bate bean
beanie bear beat beaten beater
berate beer beet bent berate
beret bier binate bine biter
brain bran brat bread brine
INEBRIATE: rebate tibia tribe.

Solution: (EASY to HARD in three) EASY—EAST—HAST—HART—HARD.

15. Postscript

What about bringing in a few graphs, charts and diagrams found in English newspapers?

— Get students to verbalize facts expressed visually in the charts, e.g. 'The number of unemployed rose steadily throughout 1980, while the number of vacancies remained very low.'

'Drugs and alcohol are a very much greater problem of teenagers today than any other problem.'

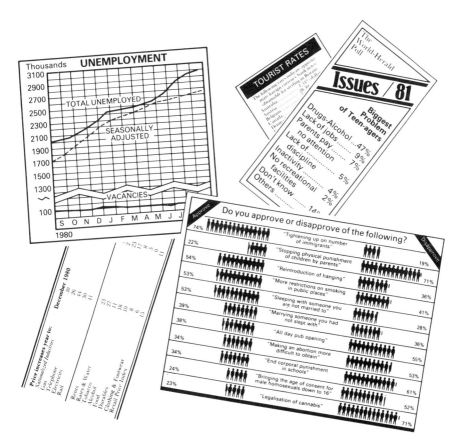

'Only 22% wanted physical punishment of children by parents to be stopped, but 34% wanted an end to corporal punishment in schools.'

— What symbols are used and recognized in the students' own culture?
— How many ways can be found for expressing a 'visual' fact?
— What kinds of information are conveyed by graphs, diagrams, charts and tables?
— Make *true/false* statements based on visuals.

Bibliography

This is intended as a guide to books and articles on the use of newspapers in English language teaching. All items are written in English and are divided into two sections:

(i) those written with native English speakers in mind;
(ii) those written specifically for foreign learners of English.

(i) Items written for native English learners

Beeler, A. J.: 'Teaching about the newspaper in elementary schools.' *Elementary English,* **49**, 2 (1972), 227–229.

Burrus, D.: 'Developing critical and creative thinking skills using the newspaper.' *Elementary English,* **47**, 4 (1970), 978–981.

Cheyney, A. B.: *Teaching Reading Skills through the Newspaper.* Newark, Del.: International Reading Association, 1971.

Crystal, D. and Davy, D.: *Investigating English Style.* London: Longman, 1967.

Decker, H.F.: 'Five dozen ideas for teaching the newspaper unit.' *English Journal,* **59** (1970), 268–272.

Downing, E. C.: *Units on the Study of the Newspaper for English: Grades 7–12.* New York: American Newspaper Publishers Foundation, 1966.

Inner London Education Authority: 'No. 2: Front Page.' *Nine Graded Simulations.* London: ILEA (undated).

Johnson, L. S.: 'The newspaper: a new textbook every day.' *Journal of Reading,* **13** (1969), 107, 112, 164, 203–206, 240, 245.

Leech, G.: *English in Advertising.* A Linguistic Study of Advertising in Great Britain. London: Longman, 1966.

Odom, N. C.: 'A dozen assignments from the newspaper.' *Journal of Reading,* **14** (1971), 475–476.

Quirk, R.: *The Use of English.* London: Longman, 1962.

Sailer, C.: 'Building reading skills via reading the newspaper.' J. A. Figarel (ed.), *Reading and Realism.* Newark, Del.: International Reading Association, 1969, 127–132.

Sanders, B.: 'MAD magazine in the remedial English class.' *English Journal,* **59** (1970), 266–267, 272.

Smith, R. B. and Michalak, B.: *How to Read Your Newspaper.* New York: Harcourt, Brace, Jovanovich, 1970.

Whistler, N. G.: 'The newspaper: resource for teaching study skills.' *The Reporting Teacher*, **25**, 7 (1972), 652–656.

(ii) Items written for EFL learners

Allard, D.: 'Write your own newspaper.' *English Teaching Guidance* (Israel), **39** (1980), 30–33.

Baddock, B. J.: 'A bibliographical guide to the use of newspapers in English language teaching.' *Die Neueren Sprachen*, **80**, 6 (1981).

Baddock, B. J.: 'The newspaper as a basis for communication activities.' *Recherches et Echanges* (forthcoming 1983).

Baddock, B. J.: 'Vocabulary development through describing pictures.' *Modern English Teacher*, **6**, 5 (1979), 9–10.

Banks, D.: 'Small ads as teaching materials.' *Modern English Teacher*, **7**, 3 (1980), 8.

Berman, M.: 'Advanced newspaper work.' *English Language Teaching Journal*, **35**, 1 (1980), 38–39.

Blatchford, C.: 'Newspapers: vehicles for teaching ESOL with a cultural focus.' *TESOL Quarterly*, **7**, 2 (1973), 145–151.

Boyle, J. P.: 'Using the headlines.' *Modern English Teacher*, **8**, 1 (1980), 4–6.

Bressan, D.: 'Crossword puzzles in modern language teaching.' *Audio-Visual Language Journal*, **8**, 2 (1970), 93–95.

Byrne, D.: 'Further suggestions for using cutouts imaginatively.' *Modern English Teacher*, **3**, 1 (1975), 12.

Carter, T. P.: 'Crossword puzzles in the foreign language classroom.' *Modern Language Journal*, **58**, 3 (1974), 112–115.

Cathcart, R. L.: 'Can an adult intermediate ESL student understand today's news?' *New Directions in Second Language Learning, Teaching and Bilingual Education*. Washington, D.C.: TESOL, 1975.

Centre for British Teachers, The: *Newspapers and the Press*. London: The Centre for British Teachers, 1976.

del Giudice, G.: 'Newspaper articles in class.' *Modern English Teacher*, **2**, 2 (1974), 10.

Fowles, J.: 'Ho Ho Ho: cartoons in the language class.' *TESOL Quarterly*, **4**, 2 (1970), 155–159.

Freitas, J. F.: *To Start You Talking*. English Conversational Practice for Foreign Learners. Unit 9: 'Talking about newspapers and magazines.' London-Dortmund: Macmillan-Lensing, 1972, 155–174.

Hampares, K. J.: 'Linguistic and cultural insights in advertising.' *Modern Language Journal*, **52**, 4 (1968), 220–222.

Hueber Hochschulreihe: 29, *The Languages of English Journalism*. A Workbook for Students. München: Hueber, 1974.

Humphris, C.: 'A newspaper project.' *Modern English Teacher*, **2**, 2 (1974), 9.

James, C. J. and Lange, D. L.: 'The use of newspapers and magazines in the foreign language classroom.' *ERIC Focus Reports on the Teaching of Foreign Languages*, **31**. New York: MLA/ERIC Clearinghouse in Languages and Linguistics, 1974.

Ketcham, R. K.: 'Studying the ads.' *Modern Language Journal*, **45**, 5 (1961), 211–214.

Lynch, T.: 'Using newspaper headlines.' *Modern English Teacher*, **6**, 6 (1979), 12–14.

Maley, A., A. Duff and F. Grellet: *The Mind's Eye.* London: C.U.P., 1980.

Mitchell, I.: 'Holidays.' *Forum,* **18** (1979), 18–19. (On using holiday advertisements.)

Mollica, A.: 'A tiger in your tank: advertisements in the language classroom.' *The Canadian Modern Languages Review,* **35**, 4 (1979), 691–743.

Mollica, A.: Cartoons in the language classroom.' *The Canadian Modern Languages Review,* **32**, 4 (1976), 424–444.

Pint, J. J.: 'Cartoons that teach: how to judge their use in ESL textbook.' *English Teaching Forum,* **39**, 4 (1981), 43–45.

Pit Corder, S.: *The Visual Element in Language Teaching.* London: Longman, 1966.

Redmonds, G.: 'The English of newspaper headlines.' *Forum,* **16** (1978), 37–40.

Sandsberry, L.: 'Magazine ads and logic in the ESL classroom.' *TESOL Quarterly,* **13**, 4 (1979), 501–507.

Taska, B.: 'Mini-lessons from the funnies.' *English Teaching Forum,* **15**, 3 (1976), 9–16.

Taska, B.: 'Mini-lessons from the funnies: a correction and an addition.' *English Teaching Forum,* **16**, 1 (1978), 29–31.

Todd, M. J.: 'Newspaper style – a practical investigation.' *English Language Teaching Journal,* **23**, 2 (1969), 138–141.

Tremblay, R.: 'Using magazine pictures in the second-language classroom.' *The Canadian Modern Languages Review,* **5**, 1 (1978), 82–86.